EGYPT

VENICE

BURTON HOLMES
TRAVELOGUES

LONDON

SWITZERLAND

1870 – 1958

BURTON HOLMES
TRAVELOGUES

With Illustrations from Photographs By the Author

— VOLUME SEVEN —

1919
THE TRAVELOGUE BUREAU
CHICAGO   NEW YORK

NORWAY

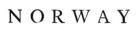

Norway

THE summer of my Norway tour seems to me now, as I recall it, like a long, magnificent dream of the impossible; a splendid scenic nightmare filled with an endless succession of sensations as overpowering and unforgettable as the scenes that inspired them were stupendously impressive. Thus in one opening sentence do I waste the adjectives that should be saved and husbanded for the descriptions of the scenes on which we are to look; yet when one tries to speak of Norway, economy of any kind appears unworthy, for in Norway, Nature herself has set us an example of extravagance unapproached anywhere on earth, save in the

Grand Cañon of Arizona, where, in a manner wholly different, she has suggested the limitless resources of her willing architects — the everlasting elements. In Arizona water has worked a wonder, and that wonder is the Cañon of the Colorado River. In Norway, ice, the elder brother of the liquid element, has performed miracles, of which the testimonies are the fjords, those terrible gashes in the breast of the Scandinavian peninsula — gashes that are deeper than the ocean and are cleft in mountains, the slopes of which descend from the line of perpetual snow to meet in the depths of submarine gorges more than four thousand feet below the level of the sea. Could we drain those rock-bound fjords, Norway would present a spectacle of unspeakable sublimity; but Norway, even as it is to-day — its grandeur half concealed by the black waters that lie heavily between the somber cliffs — is one of the most marvelous and most inspiring scenic regions of the world. To tell of Norway, one should speak a language all of form and color, light and

KING HAAKON VII

shade, and speak it with the accent of
the eternal silences that brood on
mountain-tops and in the bottom
of the sea. Therefore I pray you
to listen, not to me, but to Nature, the mother of all lands, as
she recites to you in pictured
phrase the story of her youngest
child, the last to creep out from
beneath the glacial coverlet of
the Ice Age. This Scandinavian land is the youngest of
inhabited countries, for until
a comparatively recent date —
geologically speaking — it was
covered, as Greenland is to-
day, by an ice-cap thousands of
feet deep.

Politically, Norway is one of
the oldest sovereign states of Europe,
although the ruling dynasty is the

QUEEN MAUD AND PRINCE OLAF

youngest of all dynasties, established, significant fact, by the
vote of the Norwegian people in the year 1905. King
Haakon VII is the newest of
Europe's Kings, but his
kingdom is one of the
oldest, founded eleven centuries ago, in the year 872, by
Harold the Fair-haired, who
unified the old Norse provinces
and became first King of
Norway, reigning as a

THE CROWN PRINCE AND HIS
BRITISH COUSINS

contemporary of Alfred the Great of England. Since then Norway has been united with Denmark and with Sweden, but, as we know, the union with Sweden was peacefully dissolved in 1905, and Norway then chose as her new King a Danish prince, son of King Frederick VIII of Denmark, and nephew of King George of Greece. King Haakon VII is also both cousin and brother-

LOOKING TOWARD THE ROYAL PALACE IN CHRISTIANIA

in-law of King George V, for he married the Princess Maud, youngest sister of King George. Thus the heir-apparent to Norway's throne, the Crown Prince Olaf, born in 1903, is cousin to all the little royal kiddies in Copenhagen, Stockholm, St. Petersburg, London, Athens, and Madrid. This very happy, and very royal, royal family, reigning over one of the most intensely democratic nations in the world, would seem like an anomaly. But the Norwegians are all loyal to the rulers they themselves have chosen by election, proud of their Danish King and English Queen, and devoted to their young Crown Prince, who is called "the most popular royal personage in Europe."

The most popular per-
sonage in Norway — the
man nearest to the hearts of
the people — is undoubtedly
the poet, novelist, and politi-
cian, Björnstjerne Björnson,
gentle teller of tales, vigorous
doer of deeds. The other
literary giant of the north-
land, Henrik Ibsen — maker
of those fearful, gloomy
plays — is better known to
the world at large. In music
Norway gives us Edvard
Grieg — who is, by the way,
half Scotch. Through him
"Norwegian moods and life
have entered every music-

BJÖRNSON

THE STORTHING OR PARLIAMENT

THE VRANGFOS LOCKS

room in the whole world." Another composer to whom Norse music owes much is Christian Sinding, and in painting and sculpture, Otto and Stephen Sinding, brothers of the musician, have achieved world-wide renown.

But the traveler does not come to Nor-

way to read books, see plays, listen to music, or study works of art, nor even to look at cities, palaces, or public buildings. These things, fine and worthy as they may be, are outrivaled in his estimation by the

BANDAK CANAL

scenery of Norway, which is almost without its equal in the
world.   There is apparently no end to Norway's   scenic
wealth; the land is literally crowded with
scenery; the inhabitants of some regions
find but a narrow foothold between the
mountains and the invading chan-

EDVARD
GRIEG

HENRIK IBSEN

nels of the sea. In fact thousands of Norwegians are crowded
out of their country every year. Two thirds of the Norwegians
now alive are in the United States, the majority of these expatri-
ated Norsemen living to-day in Iowa, Wisconsin, the Dakotas,
and Minnesota, and more are
coming over every year. And
the more the merrier; the
more of these good,
sturdy, honest folk
that come to people
our spacious land,
the better for us, for
them, and for the
progress of the human
race. Of course, we
should not like to depopu-
late their country, for though we
might in return repopulate it with

NORWEGIAN BOYS . . .

American tourists, Norway without the Norwegians would lack
one of the elements that lends much charm to travel in this
scenic wonderland. But there is no danger of Norway's
population disappearing. In spite of heavy emigration —
about twenty thousand an-
nually — the population of
Norway has doubled in the
course of the last half-cen-
tury, and numbers now
nearly two and a half millions. Yet this means that
Norway is but sparsely inhabited, this population
representing less than
one half of one per
cent of the popu-

. - - AND GIRLS

OLD BOYS . . .

lation of the Continent of Europe. Although Norwegians at home are comparatively poor — less than three per cent of them being persons of independent means — all are independent in spirit, all are self-supporting, there is no visible misery, there are no paupers and no tramps, and there is no child labor. Every citizen has a vote; the franchise has been extended to women, and in several Norwegian cities women sit to-day in the municipal councils. There is no privileged class. All the old orders of nobility were abolished in 1814, but holders of titles were allowed to retain them for life. We are told that the feudal system with its serfdom never got a foothold in Norway, and that the wealthiest landlord is only a peasant. Björnson says: "No other country possesses so many men in official positions — doctors, clergymen, engineers, teachers, and merchants — who are peasant-born, and in no other country

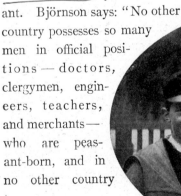

. . . AND OTHER BOYS

have so many poets, artists, men of science, and statesmen risen directly from the peasant class." A man who commands an income of five thousand dollars a year is looked upon as a rich man. Members of Parliament draw a salary of three dollars and a quarter a day! — and yet we never hear of such a thing as graft in this land of the simple life. Travel in Norway is naturally cheaper than in other countries where money is easier to get. Amazingly low are the rates of fare fixed by the government for the posting services maintained on all the chief highroads —

THE STOLKJAERRE   about seven cents a mile

for horse and vehicle and driver! — and on certain routes this rate is cut in half! Except for a few touring landeaux and victorias, which seem quite out of place in Norway, Norwegian conveyances are utterly unlike the wheeled things seen in any other country, and Norwegian horses are differently "complected" from the equine toilers in other portions of the world. The ideal trap for the single traveler is the cariole. It is like a barber-chair on wheels

THE BOY BEHIND

with a shelf behind for the small boy who drives; that is, when the passenger has no impedimenta, he is sure to have a small boy as driver, but if there be baggage, the small boy usually develops into a big boy who sits heavily upon your suit-case, and digs his heels into your pet alligator satchel, while your shawl-strap dangles in the dust between the wheels with a small bale of hay and a large sack of fodder — and yet despite its unique character the cariole suggests our favorite

THE CARIOLE

Oriental rig, the jinrikisha. It offers many advantages to the man who wants to see the scenery — the boy who drives is out of sight behind, the pony in front is small and inconspicuous — the passenger is practically alone with Nature. You enjoy all the exhilaration of bicycling without the effort of propulsion or the strain of steering, and you are spared the necessity of listening to and responding to remarks about the scenery. The boy beholds no beauty in the old familiar landscape, through which he drives a dozen foreigners each week, and your fellow-traveler in the other cariole is usually so far away that conversation is cut off

TELEMARKEN ARCHITECTURE

entirely. Of course there are times when you do want to travel by twos and to respond to murmurs of delight and admiration. The Norseman has met this need by inventing that kindred conveyance, the stolkjaerre, which accommodates two

persons — and alas, the inevitable boy. But the boy is human, and as soon as he realizes that three is a crowd he will begin to take an absorbing interest in the receding landscape. The only drawback is that you never know when the boy may be compelled to look around to guide the horse, and thus much of his discretion and good-will go for naught. He does not even have to get down to open any of the many gates that bar the road and keep the cows from straying off their owners' land — for the approach to the gate is always heralded by a scam-   per-
ing of children across the fields,
and when the gate is reached,
there are the breathless young-
sters holding it wide open
and looking at you with a
look of veiled expectancy,
that is so anxious and so
honest that it rarely fails of
its reward. You may feel
sure that even if you do not
give the usual little present,
they will still be content in

OLD NORWAY

having served you, that there will be no scowl of disappointment nor of anger — no murmuring against the "stingy stranger." We tested them time and again, giving them only thanks, still they never failed to smile politely even when left empty-handed; but when we did give the expected trifle, they would grasp it, and, in one and the same gesture, take and shake the hand that gave

SWEETHEARTS AND WIVES

the gift. At first we found it difficult, this game of simultaneous give and take, but we soon became expert in changing our small change into the hearty handshakes of those grateful children at the gates. In posting through the Telemarken district the traveler sees many beautiful and curious examples of Norwegian architecture — fanciful farmhouses, store-houses, and stables, quite unlike any rustic structures he has seen elsewhere. Along the higher sections of the route the buildings become more crude and comfortless although still picturesque. Rough indeed must be the winter life in these high, dreary regions: rough must have been the people in the olden times, for we are told that in the seventeenth century when the peasants assembled for a wedding feast the women of the Telemarken used to bring with them their husbands' winding sheets, to be prepared for an emergency, for in those days many a wedding guest was sent home in his shroud.

The traveler will be disappointed if he looks for picturesque costumes in Norway; the old-time peasant dress is seen now only in museums, or possibly on holidays or church days in certain villages or valleys; and save in the Telemarken he will see little that is quaint in architecture except the old Stav churches of which about two dozen are still to be seen in various parts of the country. Strikingly Oriental in aspect, they are nevertheless strictly Scandinavian

A STAV CHURCH

creations, designed by the Norse artists of the eleventh, twelfth, and thirteenth centuries, and constructed by the honest carpenters and carvers of those far-off medi-

THE VÖRINGSFOS

eval times. We in these days of flimsy buildings, look with
wonder and respect at wooden churches that have stood through
the storms of seven or eight hundred years and are still worth

ON THE WAY TO THE VÖRINGSFOS

looking at, still capable of revealing the art-spirit of the distant
age of which they are the almost unique memorials.

Our first tour overland is from Christiania to the Hardanger
Fjord, a journey of about three hundred miles, in the course of

which we travel by rail, by road, by canal steamer — up through the wonderful locks at the Vrangfos and along the watery avenues that wind through the mountain forests — and then again by cariole and stolkjaerre down to the little seaport town of Odde, which paradoxically lies among the mountains more than a hundred miles from the open sea and above which the great snow-field called the Folgefond spreads its hundred and twenty square miles of glittering whiteness on the roof of the broad fjeld. From Odde we proceed by water to the port called Vik, there to begin a wonderfully varied little mountain tour — a veritable *multum in parvo*,

THE
MAABÖDAL
FROM
ABOVE THE
VÖRINGSFOS

THE SIMODAL

for it gives us a series of sights
each one of which must be described in terms superlative; the
grandest glacial lake, the Eidfjordvand; the newest scenic road, into
the deep, solemn Maabödal; and
at the far inner end of
that valley, the grandest
waterfall of all

A WOMAN OF THE SIMODAL

the ten thousand Nor-
wegian waterfalls —
the Vöringsfos,
five hundred and
twenty feet in
height, surpassing
in altitude and
nearly equaling in
volume and in
grandeur even the
Great Falls of
the Yellowstone.
Moreover, this
same little
tour in-
cludes
what

DRYING GRAIN

was for us the most disagreeable experience that
we "enjoyed" in Norway, for we did enjoy it —
after it was over — the long tramp across the boggy
tops of the fjelds to the brink of the deep Simodal
which calls for yet another superlative, for it is the
lovliest of all the dales or valleys of this region.

, , , AND HER HUSBAND

MIDSUMMER SNOW

A peaceful *gaard* or hamlet lies there by the silvery fjord, seemingly almost within a stone's throw of the snow-drifts where we
stand, but when the guide attempts to throw a stone we shrink
back with a sickening sense of dizziness, as if we feared that the
abysmal valley would retaliate like an angry monster by snap-
ping at the rash offending pygmies on the brink. Turning at
last from the hypnotic fascination of the gulf we clamber over
the rocks made red and yellow with
a curious little shrub, till suddenly
a pleasing vision bursts upon
us — a glacier of green, glis-
tening ice half veiled in
snow, resting with cloud-
like lightness between the
rocky walls and filling
with the rain of its slow
melting a little lake,
the Rembedals-vand. It
forms an ice-dam that men-
aces the safety of the Simo-

DOWN THE SIMODAL TO
THE HARDANGER FJORD

dal, for in the spring two lakes form in a high ravine behind
and above the icy barrier, rising until they become one. Finally
a curious thing occurs: the surface water overflows the dam
and the under masses, aided by the pressure of the flooded
lake, work their way under the ice and then up through the
crevasses, until the glacier begins to spout like a glorious fountain

THE REMBEDALS-VAND

of a thousand jets. Thus this most curious of glaciers may be
said to give itself a bath and wash away the stony stains that
winter avalanches may have left upon it and which remain upon
and soil and spoil the beauty of so many greater glaciers But
sometimes, ere this relief is found, the ice gives way, the upper
lakes are dropped into the lower bed, which is already full, and
thereupon a world of ice-choked water is hurled over the brink
into the valley where farms and houses, roads and bridges, and
even human lives are wiped out of existence.

No vista in all Norway impressed us more than this outlook
over the somber gulf of this ill-fated valley. We stand upon the

border of a glacial lake, and look down upon the fertile fields,
divided by a river all spun of flashing foam, curving its tur-
bulent way to the calm deep fjord that winds majestically westward toward the open sea, more than a hundred miles away.
Then follows a thrilling descent into the Simodal, down the longest,

ON THE BERGEN–CHRISTIANIA LINE

steepest flight of semi-natural steps in the world, then a stroll
through the valley to the fjord, and on the following day a steamer
cruise to Bergen, the most interesting city in all Norway.   Bergen
may now be reached by rail direct from Christiania in fourteen
hours; the distance between the new capital and the old seaport is
a little over three hundred miles.   The first through-train over the
completed Bergen Railway was run in December, 1909, although

the oldest section of the line was opened to traffic in 1883. The sections of this railway near the Bergen end are remarkable for the striking frequency with which the train plunges through deep rocky cuts and rock-hewn tunnels. The new sections in the mountains lie in the region of

NEAR THE HIGHEST POINT

A NORWEGIAN LAKE

perpetual snow, three and four thousand feet above the sea, the highest point 4268 feet, and in this northern latitude this means twelve months of winter every year. Thus even in midsummer the traveler may see the glories of the Norwegian winter on his way by rail across the fjelds from Christiania to Bergen.

PANORAMA OF BERGEN

A bird's-eye view of Bergen recalls one of those pictures in our old school geographies illustrating the "physical features of the globe," for from the mountain drive—the Fjeldvei—we look down on seas and continents, islands and peninsulas, capes and promontories, bays, gulfs, channels, hills, headlands, and harbors.

As a seaport Bergen enjoys an advantage over Christiania, for although farther north, the port of Bergen is ice-free all winter. As a city, Bergen was, until the middle of the last century, a larger and more important place than Christiania, but the capital has now become the metropolis as well, with a population of about a quarter of a million, while Bergen, although growing and thriving, houses less than a hundred thousand. Bergen is enjoying still the prosperity that dates from the advent of the old Hanse traders who in the fifteenth century made Bergen the chief Nor-

FROM THE FJELDVEI

wegian port of the Hanseatic League. Those medieval merchants were chiefly Germans, and for a time they ruled the port with a high hand, imposing their will upon the native traders and forcing the seafarers of the north to bring their fish to Bergen to be marketed. To-day trade flows in the old channels, the hardy toilers of the Nordland still bring their cod and oil to the old German quay. The Hansa League at one time controlled about ninety towns, from Bergen to Venice and from Novgorod to Hamburg. The League had its own fleet; all employees were

required to take vows of celibacy during their periods of service
lest they betray League secrets to their wives, — and there were
dark dishonest secrets to be kept. For example, two sets of
scales were used, one set for weighing the fish or merchandise
bought by the League, another and quite different set for weighing the goods bought by the League's customers. Yet in their
counting-rooms were found pious mottoes such as these, "The

BERGEN HARBOR

blessing of God on the small profit," "Without God's blessing all
is vain," "Be always candid — also vigilant!" Vigilant they
were, those old-time hypocrites, whose power at one time was
greater than the might of Kings. It was said in their day, when
Norway was under the rule of Denmark, that no King might rule
in Copenhagen without the consent of the Hanse towns.

    The word Hanse or Hansa means a "troop" or "muster,"
hence a "union," and in their union the Hanse towns found their
strength and used it to kill competition and to check piracy.

    Bergen combines the pleasing newness of to-day and the not
less pleasing oldness of five hundred years ago. Even in dress there
is a range of scores of years. Beside the tall young woman in a
modern frock we see a dame of other days, wearing the dress of
long ago, looking with unapproving eye upon the frivolous in-

novations of the rising generation. The hard, firm features of some grim old faces tell of that strength of character that has been the stay and the salvation of the Norseman's race and has enabled these hardy folk to triumph over the most adverse conditions. In nothing was this force of character more vigorously manifested than in the comparatively recent campaign against the curse of drink, a campaign that has been crowned with marvelous success.

In the early years of the last century Norway was in the cruel grip of alcohol. The effects of indulgence were so widespread and so alarming between 1830 and 1840 that the period is now spoken of as the time of the "Spirits' Plague" which ravaged the nation, threatening the health, prosperity, and happiness of the entire population. The annual consumption of spirits per capita was about eight quarts; and by spirits is meant, not beer or wine but strong spirits, 100 per cent alcohol! Drunkenness, crime, and

THE FAMOUS FISH MARKET

LIVE FISH FOR SALE

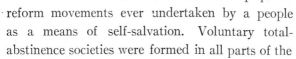

SEA FOOD BY THE SLICE

suicide were the burdens that
weighed with crushing force
upon the men and women of
the land.   In 1871 stringent
measures were taken by the
government to check the evil.
The Gothenburg system was
introduced. Official ef-
forts were seconded
by one of the most
remarkable popular
reform movements ever undertaken by a people
as a means of self-salvation. Voluntary total-
abstinence societies were formed in all parts of the
kingdom, and the new laws were vigorously en-
forced.   The sale of spirits by private firms was
prohibited, and the monopoly of the trade
given to philanthropic societies called
"Samlags," which were allowed to

WITH FULL BASKETS

retain only 5 per cent of the profits, the remainder of the enormous gain, usually about 120 per cent being devoted to objects
of public utility — road-building and sanitary betterments.   The
women of the nation took an active part in the reform, for
they shared with the men the right to vote in the matter of local
option, and in many districts even the licensed bars were not
permitted to exist.   As a result of about forty years of effort the
per capita consumption has been reduced to one eighth its former volume, economic conditions   have
steadily improved, crime has
decreased, the number of
lunatics and suicides
has been reduced,
the death rate has

TYDSKEBRYGGEN — THE GERMAN QUAY

been lowered by two thirds, and the people have educated
themselves to true temperance if not to abstinence.   Counting
the bars in every Norwegian town and city, there are but one
hundred and thirty!   Take the country as a whole, and there is
only one place for the sale of spirits to every sixteen thousand
of the inhabitants!   And yet the samlags that control these bars
have dispensed within the last few years profits to the amount of
many million dollars, for the good of the people.   In Christiania

the profits of the "booze business" go to the National
Theatre, the Museums, the temperance societies,
the Salvation Army, children's hospitals, and
vacation tours for the poor. Yet the bars that
yield these profits are operated under the most severe
restrictions, no music, no chairs and tables, no
attractions; one drink may be consumed on the
premises, one bottle may be bought to be carried home by any one over eighteen years of
age, but the same customer may not take another
drink or buy another bottle until one full hour has
elapsed. The bars are closed on Sundays and
holidays, and at six o'clock on the evening before. The purity and excellence of the wines
sold are guaranteed by the authorities, the prices
are low, and the enormous profits go, not into the pockets of
liquor dealers, corrupt politicians, and negligent policemen, but
into good roads, good works of all kinds for the enjoyment of
both those who drink in moderation and those who find a clear

MEDIEVAL BERGEN

head more exhilarating than the itch of alcohol. It is significant that there is no "club life" in Norway; there is one club
in Bergen, but — again significant — it is called "Den Gode
Hensigt" — "The Good Intention!" But Bergen is far from
being a dry town. Nature sees to it that Bergen gets plenty of

MODERN BERGEN

water. It is one of the wettest towns on earth, but Bergenites
say that the almost constant rain is responsible for the large number of distinguished men that Bergen has produced. The damp-
ness, they say, keeps the brain soft and open to new impressions.

Bergen has experienced fiery outbursts other than those of
alcoholic indulgence and of reform zeal, for the city has been many
times consumed by conflagrations. The older town was built
chiefly of wood and was so often flashed out of existence in a
night or a day that now the Bergenites leave spacious open areas
at frequent intervals between the blocks of houses to confine all

THE SUNDAY PROMENADERS

future visitations of the fire devil to an isolated quarter. Bergen of course offers much of interest in her curious old buildings and especially her excellent museums, where old Norse life is illustrated in a most interesting manner. One small world-famous thing I saw in a museum here at Bergen impressed me more than all the rest; it was the old Italian violin which in the hands of Ole Bull filled half the world with its sweet music and wrung tears of pleasure from the eyes of men in almost every country where men have learned to know the inspiration and the consolation that flow from a violin, when Genius wields the bow.

IN THE PARK

Ole Bull, born in Bergen in 1810, died near this place in 1880. Grieg played the organ at his funeral and Björnson spoke his eulogy. Five tours of the United States, one with a little girl called Adelina Patti, won for him the love of the American public. There may be but few to-day who ever heard him play, but there is none who does not know the name and fame of Ole Bull, the Norwegian master of the sweetest instrument that ever spoke to human ears.

The Scandinavians seem to be the most honest people in the world — so honest that we often smile at the excess to which they are carried by the promptings of their innate and quite unconscious rectitude. For example, let me assure you that they may be trusted implicitly to rob themselves in their attempt to treat the traveler fairly. Full thirteen times I had occasion, on paying for accommodations, to remonstrate about mistakes in change; without an instant's hesitation, the erring landlord would hand over additional *kroner* as long as I appeared to be expectant, and then I would lay all the coins down on the table and explain to him that the mistake was *in my favor*, that he had given me in the

MONUMENT TO OLE BULL — BY STEPHEN SINDING

first place from one to half a dozen
kroner more than was my due. I
can recall thirteen similar mistakes, but I can't say how often
I was taken advantage of without my knowledge, and loaded
down with surplus coin to
which I had no right or title;

for after a while
one wearies of
remonstrance,
and submits
with closed
eyes and open
hands to this

BERGENITES — YOUNG AND OLD

new form of imposition. Even a professional
pickpocket would be shamed into honesty by
the square dealing he would meet with
here in Norway. And the Norwegians are
as modest and kindly as they are honest.
One morning I had to travel fifteen miles
in order to reach a boat that was to start
at 9 A. M. The man-of-all-work at the
inn waked me at four o'clock, prepared
and served my breakfast, hitched up his
stolkjaerre, and in the drear misty chill of
the northern daybreak drove me over the
mountains for four hours, and then in a

drenching rain down to the little port, and on arrival carried my baggage to the steamer. I asked him how much I owed him. "Seven *kroner*, sir," was the reply. As that is not quite two dollars, I added two *kroner*, about fifty cents, as a gratuity, but instead of thanking me, he thrust it back and said, "That's quite too much, sir, for the little I have done — give me one

IN ONE OF BERGEN'S CHURCHES

krone, that will be enough." Match me that driver in any local hackman's union if you can!

Another instance of honest kindliness: we tried to buy a quantity of cornmeal for our provision basket; the grocer first approached had none in stock; he sent his helpers to four other shops and finally secured a two-pound package, which he delivered to us with apologies for the delay, and a bill for the equivalent of four and a half cents!

From Bergen's harbor we sail out amid the islands of what is called Skjoergaard, a long reef of islands, sheltering a kind of sound along the western coast of Norway — a sound that is peculiar

in that its channels, between the mainland and the island barrier,
are deeper than the outer ocean. Our course is northward toward the entrance to another fjord, the Sogne Fjord, the longest

A SEA-VOYAGE AMONG THE MOUNTAINS

and most varied fjord of Norway. It stretches inland from
the sea for a full hundred and thirty-six miles; it has thrust its
long fingers into the wooded shores and dug its sharp nails into
the rocky walls and there pried open crevices into which the sea
has rushed to hold the cliffs apart. The fjords of southern
Norway, the first fjords the traveler sees as he approaches Chris-

IN THE FJAERLANDS FJORD

tiania, are not fjords as we understand the word. They seem more
like long, winding lakes or widespread inlets of the sea, diversified
by low-lying points, peninsulas, and islands. The word "fjord"

is the Scandinavian word for a large inlet or a bay, but it is usually applied by us only to such as are shut in by towering cliffs or mountains. Every fjord has many fingers, thus adding many hundred

APPROACHING BALHOLM

miles to the amazing coast-line of this deeply indented land. The Scandinavian peninsula is about twelve hundred miles long, from north to south. Norway itself has an outer coast-line of seventeen hundred miles, but were the traveler to follow every indentation of the coast and journey up and down the shores of every fjord, he would have to cover more than twelve thousand miles!

IN A LABYRINTH OF FLOODED CAÑONS

To make clear the peculiar conditions of Norwegian travel a map must be consulted. We see a ragged coast-line protected by a narrow archipelago, and a rocky shore, indented as is no other

shore in all the world, for the salt sea has thrust its long and many-
membered arms into the body of the land and gripped it in a
watery grasp, so strong that even in the very heart of Norway
the fluid fingers of the fjords appear almost to meet behind the
granite mountains.   Up or down each of these flooded gorges we
are to glide, sometimes passing from one to another by way of

" A DEEP-DROWNED VALLEY "

the outer channels, sometimes scaling by road or mountain-trail
the granite ridges that divide the inland waters.   To travel for
any great distance in a straight line in Norway is impossible; we
must work our way northward in a series of long zigzags, eastward
and westward from the seacoast to the innermost extremity of
one fjord, thence up the valley, following the course of the river
to the cascade or cataract down which its waters come from the
cloudy highlands and the glaciers.   Then we must climb over
passes and traverse high snow-fields and tramp boggy uplands
to the head of another valley down which we make our way
to another fjord and to the sea, only to turn eastward once again

and work our way back into still more remote recesses of this
superb peninsula. Our land journeys are made sometimes on
foot, sometimes in cariole or stolkjaerre, posting over the splendid
roads. Our shorter voyages by water are made in posting boats,
for there is a posting system maintained on the fjords — a four-
oared boat costing only about twelve cents a mile. Longer
voyages of course are made by steamer, and these cruises through
the land-locked fjords are tremendously impressive. But the
gradual unfolding of successive scenes as we approach and
slowly round headland after headland can be portrayed only in
motion pictures — and motion pictures cannot yet be reproduced
in books.

The grandest of the many divisions of the Sogne Fjord, is
called the Naero Fjord. So deep are these inner channels that
in laying telegraphic cables they do not *lay* them, they *hang*
them in the water from shore to shore, allowing them to sag just
low   enough not to be fouled by the keels of

passing ships; it would be impractic-
able to make the cables long enough

A PORT IN THE FJORD

to reach and rest upon the bottom, three or four thousand feet below. Curiously enough these flooded valleys are generally deepest farthest from the sea. They are as a rule partially obstructed at the entrance by moraines, which are bars or ridges heaped up by glacial action, and so it happens that as a great deal of fresh water is poured into the narrow fjords by waterfalls and rivulets, by weeping skies and melting snows, we find that for a depth of three or four feet the fjord is fresh and freshwater plants flourish instead of seaweed. In winter the surface of the Naero Fjord is frozen solid and the traveler could approach on skates the famous scenic valley called the Naerodal toward which we are now cruising in a sea-going ship. In

CRUISING BETWEEN CLIFFS

grandeur the approach to the Naerodal is almost unsurpassed, and as we glide on in the shadow of the black and savage cliffs we ask what earthly power could have torn this rent in the earth's crust,—a rent as high as the mountains and as deep below the waters as its walls are high above them, for the fjord is here four thousand feet in depth and cliffs rise almost sheer four thousand feet above the waters. Geology informs us that all the fjords have been cut in the mountain-mass of Norway by the ice-rivers of the glacial age, rivers of ice so deep, so heavy, and so irresistible that as they ground their slow way toward the sea they literally gouged out these gulfs, driving their sharp ice-tools into that portion of the land that lay beneath the

IN THE NAERO FJORD

waters and grinding grooves that are in many places four thousand feet in depth, deeper even than the open ocean toward which the glacier was making its tremendous toilsome way. Moreover we know that after scooping out these fathomless and complex channels with which the interior of Norway is thus honeycombed, the glaciers, reaching the ocean edge, began a long march down the coast and hollowed out a broad, deep coastwise channel, so that the outer ocean is far shallower than is the island-dotted sound that borders Norway's western shores. Geology tells us also that the ice-sheet that then covered Scandinavia was seven thousand feet thick, that every scrap of ice was on the move, and that much of the material carried away from Norway by that moving ice now forms part of northern Germany!

In the course of our various cruises on the Norwegian steamers we learn that there are two rates of fare, one for the confirmed passengers, a lower one for the unconfirmed,— that is, for children, for it is taken for granted that all over fourteen years have joined the church.

In both town and country, religion plays a very intimate and practical part in the life of every citizen. They tell us

GORGES GOUGED BY GLACIERS

that confirmation of children at the age of fourteen years is the source of religious unity. It admits them to the rights and privileges of religious life and is necessary for admission to the civil service. A Norwegian not confirmed would not only be denied employment in the public service but could not contract marriage or assume the responsibilities of adulthood. So closely is the idea of confirmation associated with the idea of competency that we

THE NAERO FJORD FROM GUAVAUGEN

frequently see in the want columns of Norwegian newspapers an "ad" that reads like this: "Wanted — a confirmed cook."

Norway is literally the most Christian country in the world — there are less than one hundred Hebrews in the land. Before 1841 Jews were excluded from the country and had to do their Norwegian business by proxy. Norway is also the most Protestant country in the world — there are less than two thousand Catholics in a total population of more than two million Lutherans.

Norway is the most sensible country in the world. Proof? The "Courts of Mutual Agreement." We are told that the voters in towns and rural districts elect every three years a "conciliation commission." Lawyers who may be made members thereof are

GUDVANGEN

not allowed to practice law during their term of office, thus removing the temptation to encourage litigation. The commission tries to reconcile parties who have differences, and, if successful, the cost is thirty cents!

Impressed by these astonishing facts, geological and miscellaneous, we have reached the inner end of the Naero Fjord and landed at the

A HAMBURG–AMERICAN CRUISING YACHT

hamlet of Gudvangen, a place that figures in the itinerary of
nearly every tourist who tours Norway.   Gudvangen is in winter time a stranger to the sun; almost sheer walls three and
four thousand feet in height cast their cold shade on this unhappy hamlet during the greater part of the Norwegian year,

THE NAERO

but during the brief sunshiny summer season hundreds of pleasure ships, some having come all the way from Hoboken, cast
anchor in Gudvangen's port and sleep in the shadow of her
towering walls, while passengers and crews make the hurried but
ever memorable trip up through the Naerodal to the hotel on
Stalheims Cliff which commands a famous view of the best
known vale in Norway.   Almost too well known is this splendid
valley.   It has been the spoil of tourists for several generations,
and its cliffs appear as if they had been smoothed and rounded

off by the persistent gaze of travelers. We feel that we are
looking at a scene that has been marred by too much admiration. The Naerodal is like a faded beauty, retaining still her
lovely features but, with her charm tempered by a self-conscious
pose, an attitude too expectant of our adulation. We who have

EIMS-KLEV

seen the savage splendor of her northern rivals, comparatively
modest, unassuming, and unspoiled, are enamoured of their rude
natural beauty, and can give to this oft-praised and justly admired panorama only the cold tribute that we pay to every famous
spectacle that does not disappoint us. The vista from Stalheims-Klev deserves its fame; it is superb — but everybody
knows it, and this robs us of our enthusiasm. The huge hotel
seen in our panoramic picture exists no more; it was destroyed
by fire a few years ago, but it has been replaced by a smaller,

less pretentious house offering equally comfortable accommodation. The road that leads from the valley floor to the top of Stalheims-Klev is famous for its sixteen steep zigzags, up which so many tourists have made their toilsome way, walking uphill behind their vehicles, because the Norwegian driver expects every passenger to make life easy for his pony; and down which so many tourists have careered at express speed, their hair on end — on both ends at the sharp switchback angles of the road — because the Norwegian driver knows no fear, and has no thought for man or beast on the down grade. There are no brakes on those two-wheeled Norwegian traps:

THE NAERODAL

once under way down hill, there is no stopping until you reach the bottom, unless you have discovered the secret sound, which is the only thing that will subdue the ardor of these mountain ponies when once they have begun to shoot the chutes along one of those curving, twisting, and self-reversing mountain roads. That secret sound is simply "Purr-r-r-r" purred in the pony's ear; "Whoa!" acts upon him as a tonic and a challenge to surpass himself in speed; but a soft "Purr-r-r-r" brings him

to a standstill and robs him of ambition.   Having survived this
thrilling descent we find ourselves a few days later in the Nord
Fjord one degree farther north.   In this fjord evil fortunes
overtook us — three days of drenching rain were here our portion and the glories of the Loen Vand, the grandest lake in
Norway, were but vaguely revealed to us by shiftings of the
jealous clouds.   I fain would sing the praises of this mountain
lake, but lakes to win from me the celebration of their charms must
be more tactful, meet me at least half way in good intentions, and
see that I am not maltreated by their winds and waves.   But
dutifully "doing" Loen Lake under weather conditions that were
most depressing, I yet saw enough to know that a bright sunny
day would have made this experience one of the most memorable
of the entire tour.   Even as it was we shall not soon forget it—
we were caught out in the middle of that lake by a terrific mountain
storm that churned the waters to foam and threatened to swamp
our little rowboat.   As the white-crested waves rose higher and
higher, and our bailing-out seemed not quite to keep pace with the

THE STALHEIMS ROAD

in-coming of the heavy wave-tops, and as the efforts of our oars-
men seemed just sufficient to hold the craft against the wind, we
experienced some doubts as to the possibility of ever reaching
shore. "Can you make it?" we ask. Without missing a stroke,
one of our men quietly answers, "Two men can do it, if they don't
get scared," and the two men bend to their oars. A little later,

TOURIST TIME

just at dusk when the storm was at its height, another rowboat
"manned" by two women shot across our bows, driven by the
gusty squalls. What errand of life or death can have brought
two women out upon this angry lake on an awful night like
this? Our calm-voiced oarsman answers, "Oh, that's only my
mother and sister going over to the other side to milk the cows."
After that we decided we could not afford to be afraid. "For
Norge Kjaempers Föderland," so runs the national anthem,
and Norway is indeed the "Fatherland of Heroes"—and of
heroines. Heroic as the men of old are the Norwegian women
of to-day. They face all manner of winter hardships and dangers

THE NORTHERN NIGHT

and in summer, when they might rightfully expect to enjoy a little comfort and serenity, they are exiled by custom to the *Saeters*, the crude dairy huts far up in the misty mountains where they spend the long days of the short summer, tending the cattle which are driven to the highlands for pasture. The green patches in the 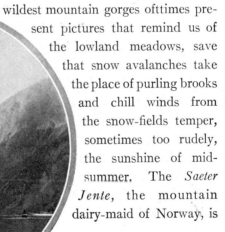 wildest mountain gorges ofttimes present pictures that remind us of the lowland meadows, save that snow avalanches take the place of purling brooks and chill winds from the snow-fields temper, sometimes too rudely, the sunshine of midsummer. The *Saeter Jente*, the mountain dairy-maid of Norway, is

IN THE NORD FJORD

doomed to live a hard and lonely life during the only season
when Norwegian low-lands are made cheerful by the return of
the sunshine and the coming of the foreign guests — the money-
spending folk for whom the poor girls
must milk the cows, churn butter, and make cheese up
there at the remote sum-
mer *Saeters* on the edge
of the mountain snow-
land, two and three
thousand feet above the
smiling summer fjord.

In the course of a long
mountain journey from
fjord to fjord over the famous
Grotlid road we spent an hour on
the shores of the Djupvand, a re-

WEDDING DANCE AT LOEN

pellant little lake, half frozen even in mid-summer, where we
found shelter in a comfortable tourist hut established and sup-

NEAR THE SAETER

ON THE GROTLID ROAD

ported by the government for the security and comfort of the traveler. It is a "Fast Skyds Station"—that is to say, a post where a fixed or "*fast*" number of post horses must be kept and where the owner must provide immediate change of horses on pain of having fines imposed for all delays exceeding fifteen minutes. There are other stations where there is no time limit set, and these the stranger calls "Slow Stations" in contradistinction to the stations that in Norwegian are called "Fast." Having almost invariably a trap engaged for the entire tour, we had but little experience with the posting system, which favors the traveler to the detriment of the poor peasant, who is com- pelled to furnish trans portation at all hours, at an absurdly low charge.

DRIVING FROM FJORD TO FJORD

The ponies are admirable little brutes, well fed, well groomed,
and rarely overworked, for the kind-hearted driver always walks
up the ascents, even when the rise is so gradual that a spirit-level
would be required to detect it; and when a steeper grade is reached,
if you do not get out and walk yourself, you must be prepared to
meet the reproachful glance of the indignant driver. Had I to
be born into the animal kingdom in the course of future trans-

THE DJUPVAND

migrations, I should pray that my soul might manifest itself in the
form of a petted pony here among these people who are merciful;
and they are as honest with the stranger as they are kindly to their
beasts, and they hold their honest services so cheap.

Cheap also are the good meals furnished at this alpine station,
and we recall with pleasure the fine fish pudding and the bright
red jellies served in this tourist hut on the frigid shores of the
half-frozen Djupvand. Thence descending we pass through a
strange region, a place of barren rock, of spotless snows, of
curious formations. The elements have labored here with tools
of water, ice, and stone; the surfaces of all the rocks are worn
smooth, well-rounded, almost polished by the grinding of the
glacier which has shrunk back even from these high places,
uncovering the curious pits or cavities, called "giant's caldrons"
hollowed in the living rock by some boulder that has been caught
and whirled around for ages by the waters rushing underneath

the ice-cap as its mass melted and passed away. These holes
are cut as neatly as if they were the work of skilled mechanics.
We saw one that was seven feet across and twelve feet deep.

But night comes on apace and we are still three thousand feet
above the sea, our destination still many miles below. We urge
the tired horses on through a misty pass, where for a time we can
see nothing because of the up-rushing of the clouds that surge

THE FAST SKYDS STATION

out from the lower gorges, seeking their resting-places for the
night high in the icy uplands where they will lie on sheets of
snow, and rest their heads on the cool glacial pillows. Then we
are conscious of a sudden downward trend
of the road we cannot see. Down,
down we go into a denser fog,
the horses almost at a run,
making with practiced ease
the sharp and to us unseen
curves, beyond which lie
vast chasms, filled with the
hurrying clouds of night.
Thus onward, downward,
for an hour, and then —
as if we were angels or
aëronauts dropped from the

FOR OUR COMFORT

A GIANT'S CALDRON

skies — we sight the earth, the solid earth, fearfully far below, wrapped in the mystery and silence of the northern night and half screened by the veil of vapor through which we are descending. Never shall I forget that vision. We seemed to wake and behold familiar things under an unfamiliar aspect. There surely is the old well-known earth, its trees and rocks, its rivers and its fields. It is the same, but we ourselves are changed; we feel as if we had passed through some curious supernatural experience, as if we had been cut off from the world, endowed with altered senses and then sent back to look with clearer eyes and a more sympathetic mind at old familiar things, to find in them new meanings and new mysteries. Believe me when I say, in seriousness, we felt as if we had been born again. Then follows a long twilight ride, down the twisted coils of one of the grandest roads in all the world, a road that leads us down to the Geiranger Fjord, a Titanic gorge, filled half-way to the brink with the waters of the wide Atlantic.

Far below lies a lake-like fragment of the sea, deep, dark, eternally quiescent, and yet a living member of the mighty ocean, for it is in reality the tip of a long finger of the sea, crooked round a rocky headland, as if to feel the pulse of this cold Scandinavian land, so recently released from the icy grip of the glaciers, that have now receded upland from the fjords, leaving that little patch of fertile, level earth where pygmy man may play at keeping house in the rude *gaards* of Merok.

MEROK AND THE GEIRANGER FJORD

Thus ends a never-to-be-forgotten journey from the Nord Fjord over the Grotlid road and through the glacial gorges down to Merok on the Geiranger Fjord. But we must not stop even there at Merok. A Norway tour is made up of glorious arrivals — and departures equally inspiring. There is no rest for body, mind, or spirit, nor do we feel the need of rest; the splendors that greet us at every turn urge us to instant onward efforts that we may see the splendors that await us farther on. There is always something finer just beyond the next bend of the road, or just beyond the next noble turn of the deep fjord, upon which we glide forward, amid the silences of centuries, beneath a canopy of cloud stretched like a thick velarium across these natural colosseums, from the summits of their huge eternal walls. Pave the Yosemite Valley with the dark waters of the northern seas; roof it with the cold gray clouds of northern skies, and multiply the cascades that come tumbling from those clouds until you have a dozen "Bridal Veils" and a full score of splendid spray-like

IN THE GEIRANGER

waterfalls, as graceful as the upper leap of Yosemite Fall itself; and then steam through this valley in an ocean liner, gliding so near the cliffs that the waters of these sky-born cataracts fall upon the decks and their icy spray dampens and chills the cheek, and you will understand perhaps the sensations of the traveler who traverses for the first time this alleyway of the ocean that is called the Geiranger Fjord. The most famous of the Geiranger water-falls is the group called "The Seven Sisters," but of these sisters we rarely find more than a quartette actually visible at one time unless we count the very little falls above, which seem more like a little colony of cousins. Just to the right of the cascades we see one of the many mountain farms that form the most surprising features of these fjords, for they are set on ledges where it seems

scarcely possible for goats to find a foothold. Yet there upon those dizzy ledges, generation after generation of strong Norse folk are born, bred, and buried, knowing no other home, looking upon the lower world as a place to which to make occasional excursions and as a market for their butter, milk, and hay, all of which is sent down to sea-level by means of taut steel wires that are stretched from those aërial farmyards to some narrow landing-ledge along the

THE SEVEN SISTERS

shore. We frequently see shining milk-cans floating slowly down-ward from those farms along an invisible wire, like balloons from which the gas is gradually escaping. Thus it might almost be said that these sky-farmers send their produce to town by wire. But the word "town" scarcely applies to the average Norwegian settlement. Even "village" is too big a term and "hamlet" not quite fitting. The right words are "tomt," "gaard," and "plads."

The average point or place upon the map of Norway is found to consist of a church, a few farmhouses, and a big, reasonably

LOOPING THE LOOP

rated and well-kept hotel, open of course only in the summer. One pays at these hotels from one dollar to a dollar and seventy-five cents a day; this includes three hearty, well-cooked meals; the best butter one could ask for, good bread, a little too much fish, some all-too-solid meat, pure milk, surpassing tea, coffee, and chocolate, and for breakfast about seven varieties of tinned seafood and never less than five peculiar and hitherto undreamed of kinds of cheese.

FROM OUR WINDOW

Never to be forgotten is the chocolate-colored cheese that always wears a bright red ribbon around its waist. Honest dealing, no tip hunting, and kindly, willing

A NORWEGIAN HOSTELRY

A POSTING STATION

service may be ex-
pected almost
everywhere, but I
must add that the
Norwegian bed-
clothes are seldom
long enough. Worst
of all, the mattress is
built into the bed in such a   way
that the sheets and blankets cannot be   READY   tucked under
at the bottom or at the sides.   The bedclothes are so econom-
ically cut that they will stretch only from the breast to the ankle,
never from the neck to the toe of the tall traveler.

Moreover, although Norway is a land of impressive silences
those silences are broken by the voice of Nature, whose lullaby,
roared out everlastingly by the cascades, which are usually located
just under your window, may soothe the hardy Norseman to deep
slumbers, but can scarce be counted on to speed the unaccustomed
traveler on his way to the dreamland that he seeks.   But later,
after he has learned the secret of wrapping his body snugly in the

A MISTY VALE

bedclothes and putting his feet into the pockets of his ulster, and when, instead of trying to bury his ears in the pillows he learns the advisability of burying the tiny pillows in his ears, then will the deep, but attenuated murmur of the waterfalls become as sweet to him as to the native who is never troubled by their thunderous song. Then, too, despite this ample supply of icy waters, sent down by the glacial snows that lie all summer on the higher fjelds, there are no adequate bathing facilities in the average hotel. It is said that even in summer it is too cold to bathe comfortably; moreover, frequent bathing is not a custom of the country. In the old pagan days every farm had its special bathhouse, and frequent vapor baths were taken by all classes, but now the bathhouse is more often used for smoking meat. It fell into disuse on the introduction of Christianity! It is said that the

"OLE

AALESUND

Christian priests and monks took up arms against the care of
the body, saying that it was flesh and represented the devil. The
spiritual advisers set themselves so strongly against the "luxu-
rious" bathing habit that the *badstue* was abandoned as a sinful
institution, and now, as a writer sadly confesses, "it is no longer
regarded as a necessary building on a Norwegian farmstead." *

Still Norway is a land of cleanliness even if modern plumbing
is not yet in evidence in the small towns and villages. The
traveler is always sure to find decent rooms, good wholesome
food, a cheery welcome, and an honest host. In seaport towns

* Will S. Monroe, "In Viking Land," to whom the writer acknowledges indebtedness for
much interesting information.

like Aalesund and Christiansund he will find regularly established Norwegian hotels, but in Molde and in the hamlets of
the celebrated Romsdal he will find tourist hotels built and man-
aged entirely with a view to the comfort of the touring stranger.

The Romsdal is one of the grandest vales in Norway. Our
arrival at Naes, the little "port of entrance" coincides with that

HARBOR OF AALESUND

of an excursion crowd of Scottish tourists "doing" Norway in
ten days in a chartered cruising steamer, that hails from the good
Scottish town of Aberdeen. Of old, the Norseman did invade
the territory of the Scot and lay rough hands upon his gold —
to-day the Scotsman invades the Norseman's land and wreaks a
canny vengeance on his old-time spoiler by forcing him to grant
painfully low rates to the Scottish tourist agencies. We trail
along in the wake of the fleet of carioles and stolkjaerres that bear
the mackintoshed invaders up the Romsdal to the hamlet of

CHRISTIANSUND

Horgheim, and then we look about us to see into what manner of valley we have come. The Romsdal is but partially revealed to us to-day. Clouds hang like torn curtains from the cliffs, and vapory masses wave before the upper windows of the valley, like draperies stirred by strong winds we do not feel. Our driver tells us that were those mountain fogs to lift we should behold the sharp serrated range of peaks called the Troldtinder, or the Needles of the Trolls, and Trolls, as he assures us, are the little monsters of the mountains, prototypes of Rip Van Winkle's pygmy mountaineers. Like Irving's Catskill dwarfs, the Trolls are famous bowlers, and as we halt to water horses at a roadside spring we hear a dull and far-off sound made by a snowball bigger than a house, that came rolling from the clouds and broke itself into a great spattering patch of white upon the talus of the cliff on the

DRYING KLIPFISH

south side of the valley. We feel like helpless ants, crawling along some bowling-alley of the giants, where at any moment we may be bowled over flat by a monumental snowball, or by one of the far more weighty missiles of the Trolls—one of those granite boulders dropped by them every now and then with frightful suddenness beside the very road. We did not actually witness the descent of any of these huge rock-masses that lie like Nature's warnings all along the way, but the pure white surfaces of the fragments, as yet untouched by time which turns them soon to gray, tells us that these playthings of the elements had shattered themselves there not many weeks ago. So imminent is the impending danger from these falling fragments of the weather-worn cliffs, hid by these almost ever-present clouds, that even the houses in the Romsdal appear to shrink from them. We saw one house, its roof bent just like the back of a whipped dog crouching to avoid a final blow. In fact, in the foreground lay the rock that probably dealt the blow that broke the shoulder of that decrepit and half-crippled house. Some of the older cabins and storehouses are

AMONG THE MOUNTAINS OF THE TROLLS

IN THE ROMSDAL

raised on stony stilts. They look as if they stood on tiptoe, ready to leap over the next descending avalanche.

Our excursion or rather incursion into the Romsdal ends at Stuefloten, which is about eight hours' drive from the fjord and two thousand feet above its level. Here another valley begins, the Gudbrandsdal, through which we could go on for days as far as Christiania. But there we turn back after a sound night's rest, and drive for a second time through this same valley of the Rauma, a river that runs, now with deliberateness, now with impetuous fury toward the distant fjord. The clouds still hide the summits of the cliffs, and thus give free play to the traveler's imagination, which proceeds to picture cliffs that have no tops and walls that have no end this side of the gates of Heaven. We know, however, that we are shut in by granite ridges ranging from three thousand to nearly fifty-seven hundred feet in height. As the day

FALLEN FROM THE CLIFFS

ROUGH AND RUSTIC

wears on, the vapors gradually disperse, revealing the full majesty of the surrounding mountains, but at the same time robbing them of more than half their mystery. We almost wish that we had never had this proof that the aspiring walls that rise above the Rauma do have a definite sky-line, like that of other mountains everywhere. But though we may regret the advent of the cloud-dispelling sun, the good folk of the Romsdal welcome his brief, infrequent visits and every family in this shadow-haunted vale turns out, and with a

A LITTLE VIKING

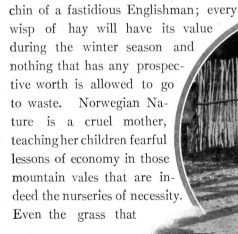

vengeance makes hay while the sun shines. If piled up in stacks the grass would never dry in this region of semi-perpetual mist and shadow. Therefore it is vigorously raked and tossed, and finally hung out upon the fence for final drying. These hay fences, called *hesjer*, are the most characteristic feature of the Norwegian landscape; we find them everywhere, drawn across the fields and pastures, like disconnected lines of some enormous unsolved proposition of geometry. Some *hesjer* are made of rails, others are made of wire, stretched on poles, but all, when covered, look like walls of hay. All Norway in summer time is cut up into closely shaven squares by these hedges of green that slowly turn to yellow as the days grow shorter and shadows

A NEW BROOM longer at the approach of the long cold winter that will keep the cattle housed and dependent on this summer crop of hay. There are only two seasons—tourist time and winter time.

Norway is the most closely shaven country in the world; scarcely a single blade of grass escapes the sickle of the gleaner, even the green borders of the roads are shaved as neatly as the chin of a fastidious Englishman; every wisp of hay will have its value during the winter season and nothing that has any prospective worth is allowed to go to waste. Norwegian Nature is a cruel mother, teaching her children fearful lessons of economy in those mountain vales that are indeed the nurseries of necessity. Even the grass that

THE GATE OPENERS

grows above the clouds is not left to wither on the slopes. After
the scant yield of the valley is securely stored, the farmers scale
the cliffs and clip the·soft green nap from every little ledge, from
every crevice in the rocks, and from the sheer green places that are
almost vertical. One must be an alpinist to cut grass in Norway.

No wonder that the young Norwegians glory in the big
farming opportunities of the American Northwest. There is but
little room for farms in Norway. Nearly two thirds of Norway's
area is represented by bare mountains; nearly all the rest by
lakes, swamps and forests, and yet agriculture is the most important industry, yielding larger returns than even the fisheries.

ON A ROMSDAL FARM

I doubt if the average Norwegian rustic appreciates the
beauties of his land. He seems
to look upon the stranger as a
sort of semi-lunatic, and
cannot understand why

WE TWO, TOO

EXCURSIONISTS AT HORGHEIM

we should come so far to see his old familiar rocks, and to travel toilsomely over the good roads he has been forced by a wise government to build. But while he realizes the efficacy of scenic beauty as a bait for foreign fools, the honest way in which he deals with them and his refusal to take advantage of their needs, when he has lured them to his country, speaks volumes for that innate rectitude which I have mentioned as the base of Scandinavian character. There is no effort to exploit the enthusiasm of the stranger; yet the temptation must be strong, when they see wealthy Americans and Englishmen willing to pay any price for the use of trout and salmon streams in the summer. The thrifty Norseman has little time to spend in playing frisky fish upon a slender line. He builds him stout salmon traps from which he lifts out every day or two a splendid fifteen pounder. The traps thus yield a considerable income to the farmer who controls the

"BERRIES"

adjacent land, but in many valleys the land-owner finds it far more advantageous to lease his river-rights to English lords, and millionaires from the United States. Many a farmer finds that the richest annual yield of his farm is the crop of coin that springs from the Anglo-Saxon love for piscatorial sport. The trout lakes in the mountains are also rich and nearly all are annually preëmpted by English anglers. We met many a dignified old Briton, who assured us that he had not missed his summer's fishing in his chosen district for the last twelve or fifteen years. From the grandiose and rural charm of these cliff-surrounded Romsdal farms we

"YA I KNOW MINNESOTA"

turn to the urban attractions of the old city of Trondhjem, once the capital of Norway, the nucleus of the nation, the cradle of Norse civilization, now a quiet city of forty thousand people.

The Cathedral of Trondhjem, half Gothic and half Romanesque, is the most notable pile in Norway. The old Norse Kings were buried here; and here, according to the Constitution of 1814, the three Swedish monarchs who ruled over the land in the last century were crowned as Kings of Norway, and here on January 1, 1906, the Norwegians crowned their own King, King Haakon VII, and his Queen, Queen Maud. Their son, the Crown Prince Olaf, is the modern namesake of the Saint and King to whom this ancient church is dedicated — St. Olaf, who was a great and good King ruling Norway nine hundred years ago. In

ONE OF THE OLD FOLKS AT HOME

TRONDHJEM CATHEDRAL

Catholic days this was a place of pilgrimage and the holy bones of Olaf the Thickset are credited with many miracles. Now the church is devoted to the severest of Protestant professions, the Lutheran, which is now the national religion of this land of the pagan Vikings and the early Catholic Kings.

For the pious there are many signs in Trondhjem that seem shocking; for example, "Rum for Resande," which means simply "Rooms for Travelers"; "Gods-expedition," which appears not over a church door, but on the side of a railway freight house, for it means "Goods-transportation." Yet even with this explanation borne in mind he is indeed an unimpressionable traveler who can read the signboard at a railway station a few miles from Trondhjem without an involuntary impulse to pinch himself to find out whether he be still alive, or whether he has died and been

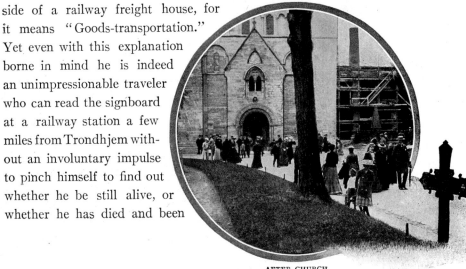

AFTER CHURCH

"THE OTHER PLACE!"

delivered at a destination that he would not have chosen, had the purchase of the ticket been left entirely to him. Glance up and read that signboard. It tells us where we are — in "Hell." It tells us also just how far it is to three other places. Fittingly, *Christ*iania is farther off by several hundred kilometers than either of the others.

It may be welcome news to some of you to learn that during our brief stop in this much discussed locality we found the weather charmingly chilly! We regretted that we had not time to stroll uptown, for had we done so we should doubtless have encountered many friends. But

TO HELL AND RETURN

as we were not expected, there were none but strangers at
the station. We were pained to note the presence of young
children, as if to affirm that revolting theory of "infant damnation."
We had not time to find out what they had done to bring them
here so early. We dared not venture far from the train,

LANDING AT TORGHATTAN

because our tickets were not good for a stop-over. Anyway, we
hadn't planned to come here — yet. But recalling the frequency
with which invitations to visit this resort are extended, especially
in English-speaking countries, we purchased round-trip tickets
for the use of certain persons who for some unaccountable reason
come to mind every time we read that sign. We were careful to
make sure that the tickets were good for "Tur & Retur," as we
might have to use them ourselves; and we took third class, because
we didn't care to meet too many people we knew on the train.
We could have had second-class tickets at a slightly higher rate,
but it is a fact worth noting that on this line *no first-class coaches*
are operated, there being no demand for first-class transportation

BEGINNING THE NORDLAND CRUISE

in the direction of that town
called "Hell." When I asked
the meaning of the name, they
told me that it signified "a flat
place" or "a low place": this
explains the frequent efforts
that are made to "raise" it.
And that reminds me of a story
apropos of those round-trip tickets
to the other place. I never thought
to buy them until the purchase was
suggested to me by an English lady
whom we met a few days later at one of

SVARTISEN GLACIER

the hotels where we were spending a rainy Sunday. She was the
prim type of British spinster, and at first our conversation was most
formal. But soon the current of our chat flowed into gayer channels, until we found ourselves relating funny stories, the English
lady easily keeping the lead with an amazing stock of curious and
almost sacrilegious epitaphs that she had copied from the tomb-
stones in many an old English churchyard. Led on by these I

ventured hesitantly to allude to Hell as a place I had already visited.
"That's nothing," exclaimed the lady; "We've been there too;
we stopped over a train to see the place and when we got to Trondhjem I bought a ticket to show to friends at home!" Impressed
by this convincing proof that English people do possess a sense of
humor, I told this story to another fellow-traveler, an English
vicar, prefacing it by saying that in America we had a notion that
Englishmen can never see a joke. "Quite wrong, my dear sir,"
he rejoined. "We are not as demonstrative as you, but we do have
an appreciation of true humor." "Yes," I said, "I have just had
this proved to me by that quiet little Englishwoman over there,
who looks so serious-minded, for she has actually bought a ticket to
that town—which in your presence shall be nameless." He looked
up with an air of interest and said, "Ah, really, she has, has she?"
and then as if he saw it, "but I presume *not intending to use it!*"
"No," I replied, "why should she?" "Why, indeed?" he mur-
mured, and we went back to hear a few more of her comic
epitaphs that we might laugh without offending.

GLACIAL ICE

At Trondhjem we book for the North Cape cruise on a Norwegian steamer, the "*Neptune*." She has but just arrived from
the preceding cruise, bringing back a band of disappointed tourists
who have sailed through arctic fogs for seven days and seen no
sign of any sun, either at noon or midnight. But undeterred by
these reports, more than a hundred sanguine adventurers are

TORGHATTAN — THE ISLAND WITH A HOLE IN IT

stowing themselves into the scarce-vacated cabins, for the steamer
sails away again this very afternoon! Every instant of the voyage
offers some detail of interest, a spouting whale, a school of por-
poises, a passing steamer, or else islands, the shapes of which may
be likened to as many things as Hamlet's cloud. There are a
hundred and fifty thousand islands off the Norway coast, and of
them the most curious is Torghattan, notable not only because of
its eccentric outline, but above all because it has a hole right
through it, a perforation through which a square patch of the sky
is visible. Excursion steamers always make a landing here,
that we may see at closer range this unique freak of nature called
the Hullet of Torghattan. At a height of four hundred feet above

A NORDLAND FJORD

the sea, behold, a colossal tunnel more than five hundred feet in length and more than two hundred feet in height and more than forty feet in breadth is pierced in the solid rock of the sea-girt mountain. That opening was once at the sea-level. The entire island has been lifted in the course of ages. Even to-day the neighboring coast is rising at the rate of one foot in every ten years. It is difficult to believe that man has not aided Nature in the making of that tunnel in the rock — its hugeness and its uselessness are the surest proofs that Nature is alone responsible, that this is the work of her untiring toilers,— frost and heat, winds and dripping waters. The hill of rock has thus been hollowed by the countless impacts of the elements, renewed and reiterated through a long period of centuries. Yet even when explained the mystery seems deeper; the why and how this thing was done is not made clear to us — and with our curiosity unsatisfied we turn in answer to the steamer's whistle and boarding the ship again we steam on northward amid hundreds of cloud-capped islands, standing like a large stock of uncalled-for Gibraltars on the watery shelves of Nature's storehouse of scenic merchandise.

There is enough spare scenery in Norway to fit out a new continent. We are in one of Nature's scenic factories; we see her products in all stages

NAMELESS GIBRALTARS

ISLANDS ABOVE THE ARCTIC CIRCLE

of construction. Here too we find her factory hands at work, fashioning the wonders that will be finished in time to delight our children of ten thousand years hence.

Our course is now toward the Lofoten Islands. During that long winter darkness forty thousand toilers of the deep assemble in these Lofoten fjords to prepare for that almost epic adventure called the Great Cod Catch. It must be a glorious thing to see the night-enshrouded waters alive with thousands of stout little ships manned by their fearless crews venturing forth upon the storm-tossed sea to wring a living from the deep. Heroic as the men themselves is their equipment — small, deckless, ten-oared boats, nets thirteen hundred yards in length, lines seven thousand feet from end to end, and upon a single line two thousand hooks! For bait they carry a good share of the annual herring catch. Surely this is heroic enterprise, this Great Cod Catch, which yields annually two million dollars worth of fish. The combined fisheries of Norway yield every year fish of various kinds to the

A VIKING SHIP

IN LOFOTEN LATITUDES

value of seven million dollars; yet a thousand *kroner* $280 28¢
is regarded as good yearly pay by the fishermen who risk their
lives and suffer awful hardships in the arctic regions.

These humble heroes are the honest, worthy sons of the thiev-
ing, heroic Vikings of the past.

We know that Norsemen once cruised to the shores of England,
France, Iceland, and even North America in little ships, not unlike
those used by the fishermen to-day — conquering the lands they
visited, founding Norse or Norman dynasties in France, in
England, and in Sicily, and infusing their vigorous young blood
into the peoples over whom they for a time held sway. Their
kingdoms are no more, but they have bequeathed us two
everlasting proofs of their existence. "Words are the only
things that last for- ever." Our word "starboard" is
but the survival of the Norse term "steer-
board," applied to the
side of the ship on which
was fixed the great oar with
which they steered their way to
the dominion of many distant
seas and shores. Then, too, the
name "Vikings," which has

THE "STEER-BOARD"

come to stand for sea-rovers, masters of the deep, means simply the men who dwelt beside the *viks* or creeks, in the fjords of Scandinavia. Their ships became the tombs of their dead chiefs. A Viking chief after death was placed with all his arms, all his jewels, and many of his treasures on board the ship he had

ALPS OF THE ARCTIC

commanded when alive, and then the ship itself was buried deep in the blue clay near the shore of the sea that the old Vikings loved so well and sailed so fearlessly. Several of these ships, a thousand years of age, yet fairly well preserved, have been brought to light and may be seen to-day in Christiania. A modern replica of one of these Viking ships actually crossed the Atlantic in 1893 and sailed through the Great Lakes to anchor in the lagoons of the Columbian Exposition in Chicago. The original of this adventurous craft, found at Gogstad, was a hundred and seventy-two feet long and drew three feet of water. The wood of another ship of the same period, when found in 1903, was in such good condition that the timbers could be steamed and bent back into their proper shape. And it was in little open boats like these that the Northmen carried terror to the more civilized kingdoms farther south.

Their first recorded foray was on the neighboring coast of Schleswig in the year 777. The following century saw them actually sailing up the rivers of the Continent—first up the Loire, putting the torch to beautiful Amboise and assaulting the towers of Tours; then up the Seine, burning Beauvais and Rouen and pillaging Paris; then up the Rhine, robbing and retreating before the fright-ened folk of the Fatherland could rouse themselves to rout the invaders. Meantime the Irish coasts were ravaged and the monks besieged in the round towers of their monasteries. 'T is even said, perish the thought, that Dublin was founded by the sea-rovers from the north, and held as a Viking stronghold for three hundred years. Then in the year 1000 America was reached —

A LAPP

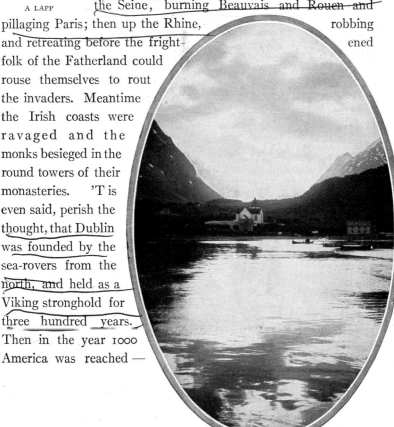

A NORDLAND PORT

Leif Ericson and his Viking crew lived for a winter in New England. The Viking age ended about 1050, but the Viking spirit did not die. Sons of the Vikings built the "*Fram*" designed by Colin Archer, whose shipyard lies near a *vik* in a Norwegian fjord, and some of the Vikings "sailed" the "*Fram*"

REINDEER

through solid ice for more than thirty-three months, when the great Nansen made his magnificent attempt to plant the Viking flag at the North Pole. Countless uncelebrated sons of the Vikings sail the seas to-day, for Norway's mercan- tile marine ranks fourth among the commercial navies of the world.

Among the dwellers in the Norwegian Nordland there are to-day some twenty thousand little people of an alien race, the Lapps, wanderers, yet ever wandering over the same desolate no-man's-land that lies between the habitable regions of Norway and north Sweden.

A LAPLAND LADY

Reindeer rearing is the favorite occupation of the Lapps, who in the summer pitch their camps near the little Nordland ports to profit by the passing of the tourist. The reindeer supplies all their needs. The milk yields butter and cheese; the fermented whey makes a strong intoxicant; the flesh is the staple food; the skins are used for making tents, blankets, coats, and trousers. The antlers are fashioned into household

utensils, the intestines into gloves, and the tendons are used in place of thread. The same

A LAPFUL OF LITTLE LAPPS

useful creature serves as beast of burden; in fact, the Lapps are compelled to maintain a reindeer posting system, like the pony Skyds system of the south. Our pictures of the Lapps, like many of the other pictures in this volume, were made long after night, or what is called *night*, had fallen — at nine or ten o'clock P. M. But day and night are terms that have become meaningless; the sun never sinks far enough below the horizon to make much difference in the illumination of the scenes past which we glide as in an endless, sleepless dream. Four hours' sleep each night is more than any of us cared to take. For three days and nights I was practically a stranger to my bunk, remaining dressed all

HAMMERFEST

night, snatching a little rest in the lounging-rooms upon the upper deck. Every hour brings its incident of interest or its striking vision of sublimity. We have allowed our watches to run down, as useless. Therefore I cannot say what time it was when we approached the little city which of all the cities on earth lies nearest to the pole. I think, however, that it was early in the morning that we glided into the harbor of Hammerfest, the midnight sun metropolis, a city of about twenty-five hundred souls. More than two months of darkness is the annual fate of Hammerfest. But for seventy-seven days, from the 13th of May until the 29th of July, the sun swings around the town, rising and falling slightly, but never going out of sight at all, save when it hides behind a hill or a house.

From a neighboring height we look down on the almost land-locked harbor, where fishing ships have settled like a flock of gulls on the blue surface of the waters, their white sails spread to catch and hold the light that is so generously shed upon this region by the long summer days, as if in compensation for the sunless days of the past winter. Beyond Hammerfest lies a realm of wonder, of mystery, where man is tolerated as an occasional intruder, but to which he can lay no claim, for he has made no permanent conquests there. And yet though Hammerfest is man's last considerable stronghold between his empire and the polar realm, we find there, in a neutral zone, a few scattered outposts, where little squads of humans do heroic sentry duty at the very topmost edge of the habitable regions of the European continent. But there is life even beyond the last of these sad isolated hamlets — life represented by the myriads of winged creatures of the sea and sky, the gulls and auks, great flocks of which have fortified themselves in the crevices and on the ledges of a range of gigantic cliffs that rise directly from the savage sea. Still,

NORTHERNMOST CITY OF THE WORLD

when we first approach that acropolis of the sea-birds, there is no sign of animation, not even the flutter of one pair of wings to hint that this indented wall is literally alive with birds. But while we strain our eyes in eager looking for the countless nests that must

WHERE THE SUN SHINES ALL NIGHT

be lodged there in the rock, the sailors on the deck are priming several cannon — an instant of expectancy is followed by the crash of a blank charge, and ere the smoke has cleared, the cliff, as if it were a feather pillow shaken by the blast, sends forth millions of snow-white plumes in pairs. Millions of auks and gulls beat the air in terror and confusion, circling and soaring, sweeping and swirling, as if a blizzard had assailed the rock with myriads of giant snowflakes. Four hours after passing the Rock of Birds, we glide past the North Cape and look around the corner of the continent. It will perhaps be novel information that at first sight of the North Cape we were not certain whether it were really the North Cape or not. Its aspect depends entirely upon the point of view. As we approached, it looked like almost any other headland of this splendid coast. There were disputes among the passengers as to which of the several cliffs in sight was the world-famous rock that we had come so far to see. There in the distance rose a cliff even more like our preconception of the North Cape. Nor is that distant cliff unworthy of our attention, for it is the Nord-Kyn, the northern tip of continental Europe. The North Cape is not a cape of the continent; it is the extremity of a small island, Magerö, set like a sentry on the frontier of the polar sea, its nose a few feet farther north than the longer proboscis thrust out in rivalry by the adjacent mainland.

The ship drops anchor near the Cape to wait for the approaching night. All hands are furnished with long lines, big hooks, and good advice as to the surest way to catch a North Cape cod.

THE LAPPS OF HAMMERFEST

My only bite was at first just a gentle nibble; then I became conscious of a slow and steady tug, a tug that grew in strength and "tuggedness" until I found it necessary to walk aft, for there was no give left in the long line upon the end of which there could be nothing smaller than a whale. Reaching the stern, the tug grew stronger still. I called a sailor to my aid

THE NORTH CAPE

to land that monster of the deep. He tried the line, then smiled and said, "Beg pardon, sir, you 've caught the bottom of the ocean." My line was entangled in the rocks and the irresistible tug that I felt was merely the drifting of the steamer. I thereupon gave up the game — the hook and line as well — and turned from frivolous pursuits to look upon the east face of the cape, recalling, as I did so, Longfellow's fitting lines, for

> ".   .   .   .   then uprose before me,
> Upon the water's edge,
> The huge and haggard shape
> Of that unknown North Cape
> Whose form is like a wedge."

The sun is still high in the northern heavens. It is still afternoon, that is to say, it is just 10 o'clock P.M ; sunset is still two hours
distant, yet had we reached this spot in June we should have seen
the sun at this same altitude at midnight. The season, however, is now advanced; it is the 26th of July; the sun sinks now
at midnight nearly to the horizon, below which it will begin
to dip again after the first of August. We are to witness its
descent from the summit of the Cape. To reach that splendid
northern balcony of Europe we must first go ashore in rowboats,
and then climb by a steep zigzag path about one thousand feet.
It is a safe but very arduous ascent, and there were few who did
not undertake it bravely. One German woman over seventy years
of age insisted that she would not miss the spectacle for which
she had sacrificed so much comfort and repose, and up she strug-
gled, aided by her friends, quite undismayed even when she slipped,
fell, and bumped her poor old nose against the rocks. With the
blood trickling down her face and mingling with
her tears of admiration,

". . . WHOSE FORM IS LIKE A WEDGE"

she stood an hour later among the younger folk upon the brink
and paid herself for all that she had suffered with the beauty
of a scene. If we did but know it, beauty can console us
for every ill that fate may try to fix upon our bodies or our
souls. But even after we have reached the top of the Cape, we are
still far from the seaward brink toward which we trudge over the
barren roof of this extensive promontory. In foggy weather
tourists would soon go astray were it not for a wire stretched from
the top of the steps across this flat, stony desert, to lead bewildered
strangers to the hut wherein they may invest in very costly bottles
of very cheap champagne, and purchase postal cards, which they
may then have canceled with a North Cape post-mark. Here
we must wait an hour ere we see that for which we are all come
so far. Mean- time we try to keep our expecta-
tions and enthusiasm as warm as
arctic winds per-
mit. Our steamer
has glided out to
sea; she lies be-
tween us and the
reflection-trail of
the descending
sun. A cannon-
shot is to an-
nounce the stroke
of twelve. But
as the sun is still
h a l f   h i d   b y
clouds, the captain
eager for the suc-
cess of our night
upon the Cape, has
ordered that the
cannoneer   shall

CLIMBING THE NORTH CAPE

THE NORTHERNMOST NORWEGIAN STRUCTURE

hold his fire until the sun be plainly seen! Only one out of four
North Cape excursion parties sees the midnight sun, but as a
famous traveler declares, "I have never met anybody who has
gone to the North Cape without seeing the midnight sun. General
absolution is granted to tourists to lie about it to other travelers
and to the folks at home."

But of this general absolution I refuse my share and flatly
state that while our little company of wanderers stood or sat there
at the world's end, whither we had come
to see the mid- night sun, we did
not see it and yet we did half
see it; for at least one half

THE MIDNIGHT WATCH

of the golden disk was visible when midnight was indicated by the ship's chronometers — although the supreme moment to enjoy the thrill of which we had traveled so many miles came a few minutes after midnight, when that kindly compromise-making cannon did at last speak its innocent untruth, announcing a belated midnight with its boom just as the full disk of the golden sun revealed itself to us between two long dense bands of gloriously golden clouds.

THE EASTERN FACE AND THE SUN AT 10 P. M.

To tell the truth about travel is sometimes very awkward, involving as it does annihilation of preconceived ideas and ideals. It is much easier to let things happen in a travelogue, not as they really did, but as they should have happened. But there is always the one auditor in a thousand or the one reader who *was there* who knows that travel climaxes do not always come just when they ought to come. It has always seemed to me worth while to talk or write for that unpleasant and accusing one — you, reader may have stood beside me when that lying cannon, unabashed by the sublimity of our surroundings, thundered its white lie in that gorgeous golden sea. But if you were there, happy reader, you will not soon forget the sight that met our gaze when at last that lone shot woke the echoes, and from the upper edge of the Old World

we looked due north and saw the orb of day muffled in golden
swathings, hanging there a few degrees above the polar horizon,
in the middle of the arctic night.

And here my tale should end, but it shall not: "A day should
be praised at night, a woman after she is buried, a sword
after it is tried, ice when it has been crossed over, and a voyage
after it is ended." The most impressive moment of our voyage

THE WESTERN FACE OF THE NORTH CAPE AT 2 A. M.

comes to us twenty-four hours later, as we cruise southward,
near the entrance of the Lyngen Fjord.

The Lyngen Fjord is the most beautiful of all the deep gulfs
that indent the Nordland shores. Through it we now steam seaward in the sunset glow over a sea of gold beneath a sky of rain-
bow radiance and between granite walls etched by the glaciers
and adorned with the designs sketched on this dull gray surface
by the new-fallen snow. Now and again the steamer steers
directly for the rocky wall, as if the snow-clad barrier were but a
beautiful illusion through which our ship could pass as freely
as she now cuts the crystal surface of the waters, wherein lies an
inverted mirrored range of granite peaks and ridges, distorted
slightly by the furrowing caused by the slow, silent progress of the

"*Neptune.*" There are no words that can convey to you the
atmosphere of this unearthly region. In fact, the Lyngen Fjord
seems quite bereft of atmosphere, like some strange region on an
unknown planet — another earth, bereft of air, of noise, of all
save color, beauty, and eternal calm. Nor are there words that
can picture the unearthliness of this region, or painters' pigments

THE MIDNIGHT SUN FROM THE NORTH CAPE

that can recreate the hues that hover over land and sea, tingeing
the rocks with unknown tints, staining the water with an unknown
dye that is as deep, as unforgettable, as it is evanescent. Every
instant witnesses a great mysterious change in the aspect of everything about us. It is as if Nature were trying, testing, strength-
ening, and attenuating the tones upon her palette, that she might
choose the most unearthly and the most heavenly, to serve as the
keynote of the tremendous picture she is about to paint for us
upon the canvas of the polar sky. At last she seems to make her

choice; earth, sky, and sea assume a
hue that is as indescribable
as it is beautiful. Mean-
time our steamer, turn-
ing her propeller with
a noiseless lentitude,
glides like some
strange, intruding,
hideous thing along
this avenue of golden
waves, toward the wide
gateway of the fjord, be-
yond which sleeps the open
ocean. An island shaped like
Capri bars the way between the

THE ALL-NIGHT SUN

two opposing headlands. It is Fuglo, a famous talisman or mag-
net for the midnight sun, for it is near that isle of Fuglo that man
most often sees a perfect vision of the orb that hangs twixt night
and day. The sun is low; it has already glided downward from
the western sky and hid itself behind the headland on the left,
where, unseen by the few mortal eyes

IN THE LYNGEN FJORD

that are to look upon the coming spectacle, it may prepare for a dramatic and effective entry on the scene.

Never was there a more expectant audience, never was a great presence more eagerly awaited. At last Phœbus Apollo enters grandly, all glorious with color that is not of earth or sky. Then follows a long hour of exquisite esthetic ecstasy. Midnight is still unsounded — we must wait and watch — watch the slow

THE MOUNTAINS OF THE NORDLAND

eastward movement of the brilliant disk which seems to roll like a great wheel of fire along a track formed by the northern edge of the expectant earth, whereon Apollo deigns not to alight. Here, near the summit of the world, the sun does not appear to sink right down to the horizon as in the old familiar sunsets we have so often watched. Instead, it glides from left to right along the horizon, its downward trend so slight that for an hour it seems to hover just a little above the line between the waters and the sky. Still there is a lowest point in the long downward arc described by the slow-moving sun. That point is due north, and as we gaze along the ship's compass we see that the sun will reach that point as soon as it has passed behind the island of Fuglo.

The sun has almost grazed the waters ere it disappears, eclipsed
by the great screen of rock, yet when it reappears about a quarter
of an hour later it seems not to have sunk an inch nearer to the
horizon.   Its reappearance
might be likened to a
horizontal sunrise —
it rises sideways
and seems to
move so rapidly
away from the
island that we are
startled, until we
suddenly realize that
our ship is moving too,—
in fact, we have drifted so far
while the sun was out of sight

WHERE DAY AND NIGHT ARE ONE

behind the island that Fuglo now presents to us an outline quite
unlike that which reminded us of Capri. Meantime, watches
in hand, we wait — all eager to assure ourselves that this time

FISHING AT
MIDNIGHT

THE SUN ROLLS BEHIND FUGLO . . .

we shall see the midnight sun at *midnight*. The long minute-hand stands nearly parallel with the short hand that marks the twelfth hour on the dial. The slow, low sun rolls imperceptibly toward that point of the compass where it should be at midnight, between the 27th and the 28th days of July. The passing of that point marks midnight, marks the end of

. . . AND WITHOUT SETTING, REAPPEARS

yesterday and the beginning of tomorrow. It marks a timeless
instant, a fragment of eternity, longer than the ages, briefer than
the tiniest fraction of recorded time. At last the cannon roars.
The sun has touched that spot in space toward which it has been
sweeping since last it arose, toward which it has already begun

MIDNIGHT!

to trend again, starting without an instant of repose on its eternal
daily round, upward and eastward, southward and westward and
downward again toward the north, ever its starting-point and ever
its destination.

Hopeless would be its endless touring, sadder than death
and annihilation and the end of everything would be this cease-
less round, did not that sun look down each day upon a world
that is a little better and a little happier than was the world of

yesterday. No matter what may be the relative advance or retrogression of our own respective corners of the universe, no matter what the proportion of sin and virtue, of pain and joy, in the small radius of our small knowledge of events, even though that knowledge embrace all that the human mind can know of this one fraction of the universe, this inconsequential fraction that we call Earth,— still must our world, as a world, be better and happier every day throughout eternity. All evil is merely retarding or destructive and must perish — all good is progressive and creative, and will endure until the rising sun shall look upon a world that is all good and always better, but never *best*, because to arrive at perfection would mean a halt; a halt would mean the end of effort, and without effort there can be no joy. The millennium begins for us the moment that we realize that what we call existence is a *perpetual progression* toward a glorious ideal, so glorious that it can never be attained, and that happiness comes only through effort. and peace only through striving toward a something greater than ourselves, but of which we are each a part, and in the glory of which we shall surely share.

7/16/97

THE SWEETNESS OF SWEDEN

The Swedish race is physically one of the finest in the world. The men as a rule are tall, sturdy and handsome; the women are endowed with a refreshingly wholesome beauty—a beauty born of simple living and of perfect health. Especially charming to the eye are the Swedish girls when dressed in the colorful peasant costumes of the land. These picturesque garments, however, are not now generally worn, but the traveler who visits the rural regions on a Sunday will be rewarded by seeing some of the young sweetness of Sweden on its way to church in the old-style holiday attire.

THE SWEETNESS OF SWEDEN

The Swedish race is physically one of the finest in the world. The men as a rule are tall, sturdy and handsome; the women are endowed with a refreshingly wholesome beauty—a beauty born of simple living and of perfect health. Especially charming to the eye are the Swedish girls when dressed in the colorful peasant costumes of the land. These picturesque garments, however, are not now generally worn, but the traveler who visits the rural regions on a Sunday will be rewarded by seeing some of the young sweetness of Sweden on its way to church in the old-style holiday attire.

SWEDEN

Sweden

THE traveler who would see the Swedes at home need not go all the way to Scandinavia. Let him but traverse the American Northwest and he will find the big blond sons of Sweden establishing, in that region of boundless promise, thousands of happy homes, wherein their love for their new adopted country is tempered only by regret for the old fatherland that has been left behind.

We have welcomed the Swede to our spacious prairies, and have sold him corner lots in all our cities. We call him a good citizen — because he does not dodge his taxes, and because he

always meets the payments on his real estate. We think of him
as a man with a peculiar accent; and beyond that accent few of
us have carried our acquaintance with the Swede. But if the
pictured Sweden and the counterfeit presentments of the Swedes
that are revealed to you in these pages convey to you the

GUSTAVUS ADOLPHUS IN GOTHENBURG

same favorable impressions that the real country and the real
people produce upon the traveler who visits Sweden, you will be
eager, I am thoroughly convinced, not only to give merely the
word of welcome, but to extend the hand of friendship to the
Swede who is our neighbor here at home. He is a numerous
neighbor, too. There are a million and a half of him in the
United States! Nearly one-third of all the Swedes alive to-day are
American citizens. In spite of the enormous number of the sons
of Sweden who have emigrated from their fatherland in "the

ancient, healthful, mountain-
ous North," to people and
make fruitful the broad, flat
places of our new, equally
healthful, and mountainless
Northwest, there are still a
few Swedes left in Sweden —
more than five millions of
them — more than twice as
many as were there a hundred
years ago.

GM
1946

Ninety-nine per cent of
Sweden's present population
is native born. Eighty-five in
every hundred are living to-day
on the very farms where they
were born. The Swedish
peasants have long pedigrees.
Their farms are looked upon
by them with as much pride as
an English earl regards his
vast entailed estates.

A Swedish farmer would
never dream of selling his
ancestral farm unless compelled to do so through some
reverse of fortune. This love
of the land,— the actual piece

HIS MAJESTY GUSTAF V

1858-1950 (92)
reign 1907-50

of land held by their fathers' fathers for many generations,— has
been one of the sources of strength of the kingdom. Sweden
is the only great nation that has never been invaded by a foreign
foe, the only nation whose boundaries have never been altered
by a successful enemy.

True, Norway is no longer ruled by a Swedish King — but   1906

Norway has never been regarded as a part of Sweden. True,
Finland was ceded to the Emperor of Russia in 1809—but Finland
was not Swedish territory; it was a separate country, the conquest
of which was begun by the Swedes in 1157, and completed in the
following   century.

SWEDISH SOLDIERS

Sweden,   properly
so called, has   always been
Sweden since it emerged as an established state from the dark
confusion of the pagan period.

In these modern days of woman suffrage agitation, it is well
to recall that it was Sweden that first recognized the equality of
women in property rights. A thousand years ago the women of
Sweden, during a fierce war with the Danes, successfully defended
the home land from which their fathers, husbands, and sons were
absent at the time, carrying the war into the enemy's country.
So well did the women bear themselves in this emergency — so
stoutly did they fight and drive back the invading Danish forces,
that the Swedish King, on his return from Denmark, recognized
their right to hold property in the land which their warlike

prowess had preserved. The gentle general who led the Swedish Amazons was a heroine, whom we like to picture to ourselves as a pretty, strapping, pink-cheeked, blue-eyed Swedish blond.

Our touristical invasion of Sweden begins at the seaport on the Skager-Rack, variously known in English as Gotenburg, Gothenburg, and Gottenburg, while the Swedes spell it Göteborg, and pronounce it "Yuteeborg." It is the second city of Sweden, with a population of one hundred and seventy thousand, and commercial and maritime interests rivaling those of Stockholm. Proud indeed would be Gustavus Adolphus could that wise ruler, whose statue stands in the chief public square, behold the progress of the city, founded under his auspices in 1619 by a number of Dutch settlers, who introduced here on the Swedish shore the urban architecture and the canals of Holland. The modern quarter is an architectural reiteration of the newer parts of Stockholm, and therefore calls for no extended description.

Gothenburg — to use the most familiar of the many orthographic forms of the name — is known chiefly as the place where

IN GOTHENBURG

TROLLHÄTTAN FALLS FROM THE HOTEL BELLEVUE

the admirable Gothenburg System of controlling the liquor
traffic was applied. Canon Peter Wieselgren of the Gothenburg
Cathedral began the campaign against the "Spirits Plague" in
1830, when the Swedish people, like their neighbors the Norwegians, were rushing to destruction down the alcoholic rapids.

FROM KING OSCAR'S BRIDGE

For the appallingly widespread drunkenness that then prevailed,
the government of Gustav III was directly to blame. Distilling
of spirits was a state monopoly. The consumption thereof was
encouraged by the state, which even went so far as to prohibit
the sale of tea and coffee. Beer and wine were then neither
plentiful nor cheap. The crude *bränvin* was consumed at the

THE "VISITORS' BOOK" IN THE GIANT'S CALDRON, CALLED KUNGSGROTTA

rate of about forty-four quarts a year per capita of the population.
Linnæus, the great naturalist, uttered protests and warnings.
The first step toward reform was the abolition of the state monopoly. Distilling was made free! For a time legalized moon-
shining outfits existed everywhere, and things went from bad to
worse. Then Wieselgren began to wage his wonderful campaign,
the result of which we see in the adoption throughout the country
of the system that bears the name of the town where it was first
tried in 1865. Bars for the sale of spirits may be conducted only
by responsible societies like the *Samlags* of Norway. All save
five per cent of the profits must be used in combating intemper-

ance. Money loaned to a drinking man for the purchase of liquor
cannot be recovered through the courts. Liquor debts are
regarded as gambling debts.

From Gothenburg we come by rail to the falls and rapids of
the Göta River at Trollhättan. Trollhättan is a manufacturing
community, but the hum of industry is drowned by the dull roar
of the waters that turn the wheels of all the mills and charm the
eye of every traveler, thus adding to the income derived from
industry the countless *kroner* of the beauty-loving stranger —
another illustration of the fact that beauty is a paying proposition. There are six separate falls, furnishing more than two
hundred thousand horse-power, but the most imposing chute is
only forty-two feet high, for the entire drop is little more than a

POLHEM'S LOCK

hundred feet with-
in a space of one
third of a mile.

In the middle
of the eighteenth
century an attempt
was made to build
a series of locks for
a ship canal at this
point, but the
works then under-
taken were aban-
doned. We see
evidences of much
wasted labor in the
deep cut that bears
the name of Pol-
hem, the engineer
who planned it.
Near by we may
study a curious

THE GÖTA ELF BELOW THE TROLLHÄTTAN FALLS

A SWEDISH WATERWAY

visitor's book in stone. The wall of a natural recess in the rocky wall, evidently part of a glacial pot-hole, has been used for years as a register on which the visits of distinguished personages are recorded. The Kings of Sweden have left their marks on that glacier-polished page, as the Pharaohs of Egypt left theirs on the granite tablets of the cliffs of the Nile. Very striking is the view down-stream, toward the lower Göta Elf, and very peaceful is the up-stream view, for above the place of rush and turmoil of the waters there sleeps a very placid river. Yet within its bosom lies the enormous power that moves the ponderous machinery of the mills, and tears the water of the chutes into the ragged shreds of forceless foam that we have seen. The real force is not there in the falls;

IN AN INLAND ARCHIPELAGO

they are but the frothy manifestations of the power latent in these lake-like waters, which are symbolical of that repose in which true power resides and whence it emanates.

It is at Trollhättan that we board the canal steamer, which has been steaming along between the fields from Gothenburg to overtake us at the entrance to the locks below the town. It is

ENTERING A LOCK

always interesting to watch a steamboat go up hill, but these canal boats are such practiced stair climbers that these low hills appear to offer no obstacles to their upward course. Into the lower lock the thick-set, rotund little ship thrusts her short body; then as the lower gates are closed, sluices above are opened and the water of the second basin gushes into the first, raising the level of its waters and with it the ship, until the water in both locks stands at the same level. Then the next pair of gates is opened and the boat advances into the second lock which, closed in turn, receives part of the water from the next higher lock, through which the ascending boat will pass in its onward and upward course, that brings it ultimately to the level of the lake-like

GOING UP

channel at the top of the long stair-way up which it has come steadily and silently, rising no less than one hundred and forty-five feet from the level of the sea to that of an inland lake. The Göta canal system begins at Gothenburg, and though we know it leads to Stockholm, it would be diffi-cult to say just where it terminates, for reaching the upland lake and river district, the waterway begins to subdivide itself, making all Sweden its *delta*, if we may so reverse the meaning of the word. Glance at a map of Sweden and you will see that this is not a fanciful statement. Apparently there is as much blue water

TRAVELING OVERLAND BY WATER

---

there upon the map as there is land, for Sweden, like its neighboring country, Finland, is internally a vast fresh-water archipelago, high above sea level. This land of elevated islands is bordered on the Baltic side by the broad salt-water archipelago called the Skärgård. An old proverb assures us that when God divided the waters from the land He forgot

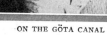

ON THE GÖTA CANAL

all about Sweden, and this accounts for the inextricable tangle of lakes and landscapes, rivers and ridges, for the watery lanes leading across green meadows, and for the mirrory paths that wind through the woods,

bringing sea-going ships even into the hillside groves, making the
snorting of the marine donkey-engine as familiar to the farmer as
the braying of his farmyard ass. To travel overland by water
across Sweden reminds one of those impossible dreams which
come to every one of us—dreams in which we are accomplishing

THE CANAL THAT PLATEN PLANNED

all sorts of curious things without the slightest sense of incongruity.
We are navigating country roads in ocean steamers, plucking
flowers from the waves of shrubbery that
break against the sides of our ship, or
promenading on a moving deck in
the shade of forest trees. Certain
phases of this waking dream bear
the stamp of naturalness, for now
and then we sweep out from the
forest-bordered channels upon
the bosom of lovely lakes, some
of which are large enough for us to

GRAVE OF BARON VON PLATEN

lose sight of land in crossing them. How any traveler can be content to go by rail across Sweden is quite inconceivable.

Wherever possible the makers of the canal have taken advantage of the natural waterways; in fact, of the two hundred and forty miles of our route from the Skager-Rack to the Baltic only

ON LAKE VETTERN

fifty-six miles are traveled through artificial channels, the rest of the way is through lakes and rivers deepened and made navigable. The inception of the plan for a cross-country water route dates from the sixteenth century, but the project was not realized until 1832, when, thanks to Baron von Platen, the Swedish promoter, and Thomas Telford, the Scottish engineer, Sweden found herself in possession of this charming water boulevard, running through a park-like country and surmounting hills and ridges by means of fifty-eight locks for lifting or lowering the floating carriages in which we travel overland.

SWEDISH SMILES

It is said that the famous John Ericsson, inventor of the screw propeller and designer of the "*Monitor*," was employed as a boy engineer during the construction of the Göta Canal and that at the tender age of twelve that young, prospective father of the modern battleship and of the torpedo-boat destroyer was ably

APPROACHING VADSTENA

directing the labors of a force of six hundred men. Did he then dream that a craft of his would turn the tide of a great war?

Our voyage from Gothenburg to Stockholm is a slow one, but so novel and so picturesque that the two and a half days pass very rapidly. Moreover, the creature comforts offered by the little canal steamers are not to be despised. It is on board our craft, the "*Baron von Platen*," that we first make acquaintance with the celebrated Swedish gastronomic institution, the Smörgåsbord, or the Bränvinsbord. Baedeker bids us beware of it; but I defy the traveler with such an appetite as the Göta voyage

A CANAL CAPTAIN

will give him to be very wary when confronted by the temptations of that laden table in the tiny ship's saloon. The Swedish Smörgåsbord has all the alluring features of the American free lunch — save that it is not free.   You take it standing up — you

BRIGHT LIGHT ALL NIGHT

can eat more in an erect attitude — and the exercise of the many reachings for delicious dainties seems to keep the appetite active. At first it is like a scramble for supper around the buffet at a ball — and everybody seizes and consumes everything in view; then, with appetites "sharpened" by the struggle, we sit to be served with the regular meal at the narrow tables — so narrow, as Mr. Stoddard says, "that an absent-minded traveler, looking off at the scenery, has been known to help himself to soup from his opposite neighbor's plate!"   The passenger himself keeps the account of what he consumes *en route,* and pays his self-made bill to the pretty, trusting stewardess just before reaching his journey's end.

By the time he has spent two days afloat in the interior of Sweden — having crossed large lakes and little lakes, having been lifted and lowered through sundry series of deep locks, and having traversed narrow canals and wide, winding rivers — the traveler is ready to believe the statement that when God divided the waters from the land, the land of the Swedes was left out of the operation. About one twelfth of the total area of Sweden is under water, but this flooded region lies far above sea level. Lake Venern is a hundred and forty-five feet above sea level. Our steamer climbs a hundred and fifty-five feet higher to reach Lake Viken, and then comes down ten feet to reach the level of Lake Vettern, which, though not the largest, is the most beautiful of the great lakes. It is about eighty miles long and twelve miles wide. On its eastern shore stands the old town of Vadstena with its feudal castle called the Vettersborg, and its old Monastery Church where lie the sacred bones of St. Bridget and her daughter St.

A PASSING CRAFT

AFTERNOON

Katrina. It is for most of us a shock to learn that there is a St.
Bridget of Sweden; she has been confounded by some writers with
the more famous Irish saint. Birgitta is the Swedish form of the
sainted lady's name. Born of noble family in the north of Sweden
in the old patriotic province of Dalecarlia, the young Birgitta married and became the mother of eight children. Her husband, Ulf
Gudmarson, was also of noble lineage. The family lived the life
of the upper classes at Upsala, then the Swedish capital. Birgitta was a born reformer — she set about improving the morals
of the court. She became a scholar and translated the Bible into
Swedish. She became a pilgrim and led prayerful bands of her
fellow country-folk on foot to holy places in Spain, her husband
and her children following in her train. She visited the Holy
Father at Rome in the year 1350. She led another pilgrimage
to Palestine. Later she founded here at Vadstena, on the
shores of Vettern, a convent for the noble ladies of her native
land, teaching them the useful art of making lace, a product for
which this town is still renowned.

But having brought us rapidly up-country, it now behooves
our sturdy captain to get us down
again to the lower level of Lake

THE VETTERSBORG

Mälaren, whose waters touch those of the sea near the stone quays of Stockholm.

One of the countless lovely islands of this lake is the summer residence of the Kings of Sweden, called Drottningholm, Queen's Island. The palace, built by the famous architect, Tessin the

PALACE OF DROTTNINGHOLM

Elder, and his equally famous son, Tessin the Younger, dates from the end of the seventeenth century. It was the favorite abode of the late King Oscar, who died in 1907.

The island summer palace of the Kings of Sweden lies very near their island capital. To say that Stockholm is the Venice of the North is to repeat a remark as true as it is trite. But Stockholm is more grandiose than Venice, and less beautiful. Stockholm stands defiantly upon her high and noble islands, resting her severely simple structures on the everlasting foundations of the northern rocks; Venice reclines in Oriental languor in the midst of her lagoons,

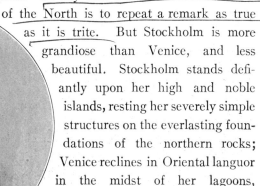

HIS LATE MAJESTY OSCAR II

spreading her complex marble piles of architecture on her low, level islands that rest upon disintegrating piles of wood driven into the mud flats centuries ago. Stockholm is clean, sound, wholesome, and modern; Venice is tarnished, crumbly, insanitary, and medieval. Stockholm, because of many virtues, commands

STADEN   THE ROYAL PALACE

PANORAMA OF STOCK

our admiration; but Venice, with all her failings, wins our love. Three hundred and fifty thousand people dwell in the Swedish capital, in a city where Nature's architecture, in the form of primeval rock, is still seen side by side with the latest creations in the way of dwelling houses, business blocks, palaces, or theaters designed and built by man. Stock-

LOOKING TOWARD THE NATIONAL MUSEUM

holm, I should say, is the most *natural* great city in the world. Nature has not been driven from the site. The ancient rocks still show their naked shapes amidst the artificialities of urban improvements, and the ancient great salt sea still heaves its living breast beneath the windows of the royal palace and the

THE RIKSDAG
1 THE GRAND HOTEL
THE ROYAL OPERA

Grand Hotel in the very midst of the metropolis. Stockholm might be called also the Paris of the North. No other northern capital can boast so much of elegance, nor reveal a finer

MEDIEVAL STOCKHOLM. FROM AN OLD PRINT

SWEDISH TORPEDO BOATS

regard for the amenities
of life — for all those
little refinements of
dress and manner, those
little ways of doing

A LOCAL FERRY

things in the most
graceful or gracious
way, which distin-
guish the city by
the Seine. Stock-
holm has the finish
and *finesse* of a
Latin city, com-
bined with the
freedom and the
frankness of the

IN STOCKHOLM HARBOR

Scandinavian north. The stranger realizes that he has reached the center of a fine civilization the moment that he enters his hotel. There is nothing like a perfectly prepared and exquisitely served dinner to convince a man of the high state of the civilization into which he has plunged on arriving in the Swedish capital. Various little touches about the appointments of his

THE GRAND HOTEL IN STOCKHOLM

room attest the elegant up-to-dateness of the establishment. Instead of a common telephone fixed to the wall in an inconvenient corner, he finds an elaborate and decorative instrument on a broad, beautifully decorated library table, at which he may sit at ease while calling up his friends to tell them that he has come to town. One very pleasant impression of the perfect organization of all things in Sweden I never shall forget. I had telegraphed my Paris bankers to send some money to meet me here in Stockholm. The expected draft was not awaiting me, but the morning after my arrival I was roused at eight o'clock by a distinguished-looking individual in a handsome

ONE OF THE BROAD QUAYS

uniform, who marched into my room, saluted me with military
éclat, and said in excellent English: "I come, sir, to give you
money," thereupon placing on the bed in which I lay a thick
packet of Swedish bank-notes. Taking my receipt and again
saluting, he retired as majestically as he had come. No question
of identification. He seemed to know his business. In happy
dreams I seem to see that Swedish
bearer of glad tidings saluting me
and saying those sweetest of all
the words in the language,
"I come, sir, to give you
money." Accordingly, with
money in our purse, we
go forth to see the sights
of Stockholm, turning to
the left along the broad
and splendid quay, called
—heaven save the typo-
graphical compositor —Södra

IN THE GRAND HOTEL

Blasieholmshamnen, along which we make our way to the
National Museum, a modern pile of greenish marble, not unlike
a Venetian palace in design. It contains collections of great
historic and artistic value, and in a garden close at hand stands
one of the most striking art works in all Sweden, one that has

THE SKEPPSBRO, OR SHIP QUAY

also an historic interest, for it illustrates one of those savagely
heroic episodes of the primitive Scandinavian past, a "belt duel."
This superb group in bronze, the work of the Swedish sculptor
Molin, pictures the most thrilling instant of one of those fierce
Viking duels, in which the combatants, bound together by the
stout belts about their waists, fight with knives until one of the
splendid human forms hangs limp and lifeless from that leathern
bond that binds it to the quivering body of the breathless, bleed-
ing victor.

Yet, lest we be carried away by that elemental admiration for mere brute courage and physical prowess that is innate in us all — half-civilized savages that we are — the sculptor, to make his work convey the fullness of the lesson it is designed to teach, has added four reliefs on four sides

of the pedestal.
The first WHERE SHIPS MOOR UNDER THE ROYAL WINDOWS of these shows the two old-time Scandinavian quarrelers at drink. The legend reads: "Not so good as they say it is, is ale for the sons of men; for the man knows in his mind always less the more he drinks." Another introduces the eternal feminine, and

NEARLY A WHEELLESS CART

bears the legend: "Mighty love makes fools of wise sons of men." The third shows the inception of the fight, when, as the inscription says, "They drew the knife out of the sheath, to the satisfaction of the evil spirit." And the last picture shows us the lamenting

THE NATIONAL MUSEUM

BALTESPANNARE

woman over whom the men have fought, exclaiming, "Solitary am I become like the aspen in the grove; poor in relations as the fir in branches." Turning from the bronze record of old-time strife and passion, we gaze across the inner harbor of the Saltsjön toward the Island of Staden on which rises the Royal Palace — and the smaller island called Helgeandsholm, apparently completely covered by the new enormous

THE BELT DUELISTS

buildings of the Riksdag, or National Diet, and the Riksbank, or National Bank. The Diet, or Parliament, consists of two chambers. There is the First Chamber, corresponding to a Senate, with a hundred and fifty members elected for six years by the twenty-five Landstings, or provincial representations, and the municipal corporations of the towns and cities. There

THE NEW RIKSDAG OR PARLIAMENT BUILDING

is a Second Chamber, corresponding to a House of Representatives, with two hundred and thirty members elected for three years, by universal suffrage, every Swede over twenty-four years of age being free to vote. There is a Council of State, corresponding to a cabinet of ministers, who act as advisers to the King and are responsible for the acts of the government. The assent of the King is necessary before any measure passed by the Diet can become a law. The National Bank belongs absolutely to the State. The directors are elected by the Diet, and the President is designated by the King. The State owns practically nearly all of the railways existing in Sweden—about eight thousand miles.

THE STRÖMPARTERRE, THE RIKSDAG, AND THE NORRBRO

THE ROYAL OPERA

One of the best points of view whence to survey the splendid urban panorama presented by this part of Stockholm is the terrace of the Royal Opera House, on which in summer an open-air café is installed. Thence we may look down on another open-air café just over the water on the Strömparterre — the flower garden laved by the Norrström, or North Stream, that rushes under the Norrbro, or North Bridge, from the fresh Lake Mälaren into the salty Saltsjön, which might be described as an urban fjord — a finger of that marine hand with which the sea has reached inland and grasped one half of Stockholm, just as Lake Mälaren has with fresh-water fingers gripped the other half. Swedish summers are not seasons of soft, balmy breezes, and to enjoy a summer evening at an out-of-door

GUSTAVUS ADOLPHUS

café or concert garden calls for an amount of warm-blooded vigor possessed by few travelers hailing from milder climes. Even the Swedes themselves find their summer nights too cool for comfort, but as summer is a fleeting luxury they make the most of it, and defy pneumonia on the benches of the Strömparterre, or at the   tables of Hassel-   backen,

or at the   Opera Café.
However, they are   THE OPERA TERRACE AND CAFÉ   not ashamed to take precautions. As the band plays on and the long evening waxes colder — but never darker, for the sunset glow lingers in the west until the glow of sunrise tints the east — and as the warm-ing faculty of arrac punch proves less and less to be relied upon, the shivering patrons of these open-air resorts at last make a reluc-tant sign to the nearest waiter, who forthwith produces that for which we, too, have been longing but never dreamed could be forthcoming at a fashionable café.   The thing of which I speak — and for which every out-door reveler in Sweden should ask early in the evening — is nothing more absurd nor less desirable than a big red blanket, furnished free by the management of the estab-

lishment. By ten P. M. the crowds at Stockholm concert gardens
and cafés suggest conclaves of blanketed Navajos waiting the
signal to begin a wild western war-dance. No self-respecting
Swede thinks of wearing an overcoat in August — not when a
big red blanket may be had in which to wrap himself and his best
girl as they sit side by side on the cold terrace of some "swell
café," and listen to the band in the pale, chilly daylight of the
northern evening hours.

The Norrbro is the focal point of Stockholm life. It is the
principal avenue of communication between the busy, modern,
commercial quarters of the Norrmalm, and the old, closely built
cradle of the capital — the Island of Staden, on which we find
a maze of very narrow, medieval streets, a few fine churches,
many historic edifices, and the enormous and imposing Royal
Palace, looming in simple rectangular majesty above the broad
granite quays which we may reach by crossing the busy North
Bridge.

GARDEN OF CHARLES XII FROM THE OPERA TERRACE

Daily at noon there passes over this same bridge a short procession of the soldiers of the palace guard. It is one of the events of the day, and, warned by distant sounds of martial music, crowds always assemble on the terrace of the palace, where we, too, take up our position to watch the marching troops go by. Oh, the thrill that answers to a burst of military music! May we never

GUSTAVUS ADOLPHUS SQUARE, THE NORRBRO AND THE PALACE

grow too old to know that strong responsive feeling roused in the breast of the small boy by sounding brass and roaring drum and clashing cymbal. There is for most of us in a swinging military march a certain satisfaction that even symphonies can never give. Symphonies speak to the highly civilized and complex soul; marches wake within us the old brute energies and send the blood coursing faster through the veins, and the healthy vibration stirred by a rousing military band is like a tonic to the senses; it prepares us to enjoy all the more completely the messages of hope and consolation found in the great tone poems which can be uttered only by that most wonderful of voices,—the voice of a great modern orchestra.

"OH, LISTEN TO THE BAND!"

The gigantic quadrilateral Royal Palace marks the site of an ancient Viking stronghold. In the year 1255 a mighty chieftain, Birger Jarl, fortified this and the neighboring islands and made Stockholm the capital of his dominions, and it has ever since remained the seat of the Swedish monarchy. The palace dates from 1760, and owes its design to Nicodemus Tessin the Younger, though it was completed by his son, who was both architect and diplomat, the third distinguished man to bear the Tessin name —a name that has been given to the style originated by Tessin the Elder, who,

THE PASSING OF THE PALACE GUARD

THE "LION TERRACE" OF THE PALACE

though of German origin, became the father of Swedish architecture. The palace contains a superb museum of arms, armor,
and costumes, many of them worn by the rulers of the past.
The state apartments of the Swedish sovereigns are, like the show
rooms of other Kings in other capitals, distinguished by the

SERVING THE
KING

presence of much that is magnificent and meaningless, and the private apartments by the usual absence of all that makes for modern comfort or convenience. Elegant is a word much abused; it has come to stand for things that are elaborate and tasteless, and in this corrupted sense of the word the palace furnishings are indeed most elegant. Many of the apartments are furnished in worse taste, with less idea of comfort, and with a more glaring tawdriness than the average continental boarding-

ON THE NORRBRO

house. If the new apartment buildings of Stockholm were as ill appointed as the royal palace, the owners could never count

THE ROYAL RESIDENCE IN STOCKHOLM

THE PALACE FAÇADE ON THE SLOTTSBACKEN

upon renting the flats to any discriminating tenant. We were completely at a loss to understand why royal inmates, possessed of royal incomes, could be content with what a commoner of moderate means would not for a moment tolerate. A friend

AT THE ROYAL GATES

ventured an explanation; it was that being royalty, royalty
visits only royalty, lodging only in the palaces of Europe, uni-
versally comfortless; thus royalty does not really know what
comfort is, nor in what genuine elegance consists. The disregard
of proper heating apparatus, the over-muchness of garish,

IN THE PALACE OF THE SWEDISH KINGS

threadbare but richly gilded furniture, the absence of plumbing,
bath-rooms, elevators, and electric buttons, — these are not
national peculiarities, as is proved by the admirable equipment of
many modern Stockholm structures; these are royal preroga-
tives. Discomfort is dominant in practically all the palaces of
Europe; for royalty, dwelling apart from the people and therefore from progress, has no inkling of the modern blessings
enjoyed by humble folk. Royalty is still surrounded by the
pomps and vanities and the crudities of the Middle Ages.

The reigning King of Sweden, Gustaf V, is the fifth sovereign of the House of Ponte Corvo, great-grandson of the founder of that house, the French soldier of fortune, Marshal Bernadotte. In the year 1810 Sweden was looking for an heir apparent. The King Charles who bore the unlucky number XIII was old and childless. Napoleon's marshals had in several cases proved themselves more than Kings, and Sweden offered one of them the crown if he would permit himself to be adopted by their

HER MAJESTY QUEEN VICTORIA OF SWEDEN   King, and to be converted to their Lutheran faith.   Marshal Bernadotte naturally accepted their kind invitation and having, as Crown Prince of Sweden, turned his sword successfully against Napoleon in 1813, he ascended the throne in 1818 as Charles XIV John. Since his death four of his descendants have reigned as Kings

THEIR ROYAL HIGHNESSES PRINCE
GUSTAF-ADOLF   AND
PRINCE SIGVARD

of Sweden, for he was succeeded by his son Oscar I; he by his son Charles XV, who was succeeded by his brother Oscar II, father of Gustaf V, who became King in 1907. The consort of the reigning sovereign is Queen Victoria, daughter of the Grand Duke of Baden. His son, the Crown Prince Gustaf-Adolf, Duke of Scania, born in 1882, married in 1905 the Princess Margaret Victoria of Connaught, niece of Edward VII of England. Their children, the little princes Gustaf-Adolf and Sigvard, smiling at you from these pages, give assurance that the dynasty of Bernadotte can count upon supplying Swedish Kings as long as the Swedes are content with a government that practically amounts to an hereditary presidency.

There is an hereditary nobility in Sweden, many of its members holding large estates, but we are told that the peasantry owns about three fourths of the pro-ductive land. The following lines from von Heidenstam's interesting study of Swedish life set forth the situation so clearly that we cannot do better than recall them here: "The freehold peasant and the land-owning nobleman are indeed the two powers that have made Sweden, and rule it. Between them they founded the monarchy — a mixture of

HIS MAJESTY KING GUSTAF V

quasi-autocratic and free republican institutions. Together they
shaped its history and molded its constitution; proudly aristocratic and ultra-democratic at one and the same time; and of the
two it is the peasant who has the better part of the partnership and
the lion's share of the power. There are over a hundred of these
freehold peasants in the Riksdag at the present moment, and
some of its best orators and cleverest debaters are to be found
among them. The Swedish nobleman has had so large a share
in Sweden's former greatness and subsequent development that
his influence remains a traditional dogma in the minds of the
people. But the peasant knows that no great decision in regard
to the government of his country has ever been taken without his
co-operation, and he is equally jealous of his traditional authority;

moreover, he
knows how to use
it, representing as
he does a majority
of the electors."

We are told
that the members
of the Diet, sent
to represent the
famous province
of Dalarne, pro-
verbially the home
of independence
and the cradle of
Swedish liberty,
are so intensely
democratic in
spirit that they
will not deign to
use titles in ad-
dressing members

THE CROWN PRINCESS MARGARET AND HER CHILDREN

men truths for which the race is not yet ripe.   But it is in the realm
of the practical that Swedish genius most conspicuously mani-
fests itself.   Linnæus in natural history, the Ericssons in engineer-
ing, Scheele in chemistry, Nordenskjöld, Nansen and Sven Hedin
in exploration, are all names that will thunder down the ages —
while the name of Nobel will ever be associated with the thunder-
ing of the dynamite that he invented.   Having found the secret
of the most destructive product of which the world is yet aware,
the thing that makes war even more terrible than it has ever been,
Alfred Nobel devoted his influence and fortune to the cause of

DROTTNING GATAN, THE PRINCIPAL SHOPPING STREET

peace. We know that one Nobel peace prize went to Theodore Roosevelt as a reward for his efforts in bringing to a close the war between Japan and Russia. There are five Nobel prizes awarded annually. The fund founded by Alfred Nobel with the fortune made in the manufacture of dynamite amounts to about eight million dollars. The annual prizes amount to over forty thousand

OLD HOUSES IN THE STADEN

dollars each. The prize in physics has been bestowed, of course, upon the discoverer of the Röntgen rays, and upon the discoverers of radium. The prize in chemistry has gone from year to year to those who have made the most important and valuable researches. The medical prize, to men who have done the most to put an end to pain, among them, of course, Finsen of the Finsen rays. The literary prize has gone at various times to men of various nationalities who have written the worthiest works: recently Selma Lagerlöf herself received it. The peace prize has been awarded to those whose efforts have done most to hasten the era of universal peace. These words of the testator, who died in 1896, give us a clear conception of his object in establishing these noble Nobel prizes:

alfred Nobel
1833-96 (63)

"I would not leave anything to a man of action or industrial enterprise; the sudden acquisition of a fortune would probably only damp the energy and weaken the spirit of enterprise of such a man. I want to aid the dreamer, the scientific enthusiast, who forgets everything in the pursuit of his idea."

Mr. Roosevelt, in accepting the peace prize, may have resented the inference that he was not a man of action, but consoled himself with the knowledge that the last phrase of the above declaration placed him among those eligible for the honors and benefits which are conferred by a Nobel prize.

STADEN STREETS

There are three of the earlier Kings of Sweden whose names convey a meaning even to the most casual student of history. They are Charles the Twelfth, Gustavus Adolphus, and Gustavus Vasa, whose statue, standing before the old Riddarhus, reveals him as a very kingly personage in splendid coronation robes, scepter in hand, altogether a most picturesque and noble figure, well in harmony with the dignified façade of the old Hall of the Knights that rises on one side of the square, in the midst of which Gustavus Vasa poses with the air of a bronze deity. This King, however, was no mere figurehead, no mere rack on which to hang elaborate robes of state. He was in the full sense of the word a King, for though they tell us now that Carlyle was wrong in saying that King means "the man who can," the man who is *able* — Gustavus Vasa became King by virtue of his power to *do*. He rose to power amid the troublous times, early in the sixteenth century, when the

THE KATARINA HISSEN

THE SLUSSEN OR SLUICE BRIDGE AND THE STADEN FROM THE KATARINA HISSEN

THE RIDDARHUS OR HALL OF THE CAVALIERS

Danish King, Christian the Second, ruled over all of Scandinavia, terrorizing his subject states by those deeds of cruelty of
which the most atrocious was the massacre of more than eighty
of the most eminent men of Sweden. That massacre, called the
Blood Bath, occurred in the old market called the Stor Torg,
in the midst of a maze of narrow streets of which a few still
remain on the Island of Staden. Among the victims of
that so-called execution, which was in fact a public carnival of murder, one of the most prominent and most
lamented was the father of Gustavus Vasa. The son
took up the sword. He roused the peasantry of Dalecarlia, the very heart of the Swedish fatherland,
where, in his youth, he had worked on the farms and
in the mines. Supported by a patriotic army, he
marched against the Danish tyrant,
captured Stockholm in 1523, dissolved the Union of Kalmar
which had bound Norway and

GUSTAVUS VASA

THE ACADEMY OF THE FINE ARTS

Sweden to the Danish monarchy, and was elected King by the
people of the land he had delivered.　He then espoused the Protestant cause, and established the Reformation in his dominions.

The Gustavus best known to us was the grandson of this

THE RIDDARHUS GARDEN FROM THE STREAM

liberator, Gustavus Adolphus the Great, who lived and fought and died a century later. He was the greatest champion of the Reformation, and under him Sweden played a noble part, her army saving the states of northern Europe from a return into the medieval darkness from which they had so recently emerged.

Thanks to Gustavus Adolphus and his Swedish legions, Europe

THE VASA BRIDGE AND THE STATUE OF OXENSTJERNA FROM THE RIDDARHUS

was delivered from the lawless armies of the brilliant but untrustworthy Wallenstein, who while fighting for the cause of the Holy Roman Empire, in the Thirty Years' War, was ever ready to treat with Protestant princes to insure himself in continued possession of his own estates. In the last great battle between these great antagonists, the Swedes, although they won the day, lost their great King, and Progress lost a champion when Gustavus Adolphus fell on the field of Lützen in 1632.

The third familiar name in the long list of Swedish Kings is that of another brilliant military monarch, Charles the Twelfth, who was called to the throne at the age of fifteen, and who, though he died in battle at the age of thirty-six, had yet found time in his short life to invade Denmark, Poland, and Russia, and to meet with a glorious defeat at the hands of his illustrious contemporary, Peter the Great, at Pultava, in 1709.

THE ROYAL
MAUSOLEUM

GUSTAVUS
VASA

THE RIDDARHOLM CHURCH

This, however, did not close his sensational career. Escaping to Turkey, he remained four years as the unwelcome guest of the Sultan, who, like a true Moslem, would not disregard the laws of hospitality until authorized by his religious advisers to lock up the dangerous visitor who was continually intriguing. But escaping from Turkey, the undaunted Charles returned to Sweden, where he organized an invasion of Norwegian territory, and was shot dead while directing the labors of his men upon the earthworks before the fort of Fredrikshald, in 1718.

CHARLES XII

He sleeps to-day with other Swedish Kings in the Riddarholm Church, which has served as a royal mausoleum since the reign of Gustavus Adolphus. There in that old Franciscan sanctuary lie the Protestant rulers of a land which until Gustavus Vasa's successful insurrection had been subject to the Catholic Kings of Denmark. To-day practically the entire population is Protestant. Statistics give only fifty-seven thousand Dissenters, twenty-five hundred Catholics, four thousand Jews, and fifty-one Mormons, and over five million Evangelical Lutherans! There is, of course, perfect religious liberty; no civil disabilities are attached to those who do not profess the national creed.

The Swedes are a well-educated people. Illiteracy is almost unknown. There are several splendid universities, one of them, that of Upsala, ranking as one of the oldest in Europe, having been founded in 1477. Over the door of the Upsala University we read the following words:

"To think freely is a great thing, To think rightly is a greater."

Upsala was in early centuries the sacred place of the old

A SWEDISH KASERN

pagan faith, of which the chief deities were Odin, Thor, and Freya.   The Swedish army has a total peace strength of about thirty-seven thousand men, and there is a well drilled militia called the *Landstorm* —not a bad name for an army, by the way — that would bring the number of men ready for effective military operations up to about two hundred thousand.   The Swedish navy is practically a home-staying navy.   For some years previous to 1904 it did not possess a single sea-going craft, all warships being of one type: low, light-draft armoured vessels, perfectly adapted to the navigation of the inland archipelagoes of Sweden.

STOCKHOLM POLICE-MEN . . .

In Sweden, as in Russia, the most imposing personages in view are the police.   But here we are not conscious of that feeling of being objects of suspicion; instead of the sudden side-glance of the Russian that gives the traveler an involuntary guilty feeling whenever he attracts police attention, we meet the square and open stare of unsuspicious eyes, which seem ever ready to acknowledge the greeting of the stranger, for there is something benign and cordial in the faces of all Swedes.

In the matter of modern scientific conveniences, Sweden is not only up-to-date but in some respects up-to-day-after-to-morrow.   The telephone system of Stockholm has long been re

. . . ARE AS DISTINGUISHED LOOKING AS FIELD-MARSHALS . . .

STATUE OF BERNADOTTE FROM
THE SLUICE BRIDGE

garded as the most
complete and best ad-
ministered in Europe.
Even at the time of
our first visit in 1902
there were sixty thou-
sand phones in use —
one for every five of
the inhabitants; that
would mean one in
every house or flat
throughout the entire
city. Nor must one
be a householder or
even enter a house to
enjoy the pleasures of
a conversation with an

. . . OR EMPERORS

THE TELEPHONE TOWER

unseen friend. The lonely stroller in the street has but to step into one of the open-work automatic telephone booths which are found at nearly every corner, drop a coin in the slot, and find himself in instant communication with almost any individual in this telephonic town. The tower of the Central Exchange is the most conspicuous land-

mark, or rather skymark, of the city. Its curious hollow form rises from a hilltop like the black skeleton of some medieval castle, and from it radiates a world of wires, like nerves from the nerve centers of a human brain. It looms there like some uncanny thing created by the thoughts that flash through it by hundreds every second. Thus it might be regarded as a fantastical illustration of the theosophical theory that thoughts do create forms that are visible to astral

A WELL-VENTILATED BOOTH

sight. Why should we be unwilling to believe in the things we cannot see? Do we not know how blind we are even to physical phenomena? Think, for example, what the trained sight of a man like the great Swedish botanist, Linné or Linnæus, whose statue we admire in one of the city parks, could discern in

MODERN STOCKHOLM

Nature. We know that to the master-minds in every branch of scientific research much that we call invisible and non-existent is visible and does exist. The fault is in ourselves, not in the universe, if we are blind to many of the grandest of physical and psychic truths.

The suburbs of Stockholm are scattered about a watery wilderness, endowed with all the charms of the forest-covered mountain and the salty sea. Within ten minutes' sail from the business center of the city the tired worker finds repose amid the wild beauty of the primeval forest, the grandeur of land-locked fragments of

SUBURBAN STOCKHOLM

a northern ocean, and the savage crudity of rock-bound coasts,

CITIFIED VIKINGS

all tempered, softened, and civilized by the labor and the care of man. No city in the world possesses such a residential region. These Stockholm suburbs are unique, and he who has not seen these ocean-circled islands that surround the city knows not

Stockholm's chief claim to distinction among the cities of the world. Not that the homes that nestle on these wild shores are magnificent; far from it; they are usually very simple, some quite plain. Display is manifested only along patriotic lines, for never have I seen so many national emblems flying as in the course of a long Sunday sail around the nearer fjords. Every loyal householder tries to surpass his neighbor in the number and the newness of his flapping flags. The entire region is alive with fluttering fields of yellow, blue, and white, as if in celebration of a holiday. It is a holy day, *Lorsday*, Lord's Day, and the

HUMBLE HOLIDAY HOMES

ONE OF THE HAPPY ISLES

OFF FOR THE ISLANDS. PONTOON PROMENADES

Swedes express their thankfulness for all the good things of this life by going forth into the woods or out on the waters to enjoy the gifts of God, to breathe fresh air, to drink sunshine, to fill the soul with gladness and the heart with love. Rowboats and sail-boats dart about the fjords; family parties sit on shore or terrace watching the cruising carnival, or walk from isle to isle over the floating bridges. They pause in smiling groups to watch our little steamer as it glides through the opening made by displacing one of the pontoons. Restaurants and holiday resorts

A FLOUR MILL

abound in the remoter parts of this domesticated archipelago.
The most popular and prettiest establishment is at Saltsjöbaden,
where thousands of pleasure seekers come to spend the day on
Sundays, and where scores of the more leisurely spend an entire
summer, enjoying the salt-water baths,
boating, fishing, and the comforts
of an excellent hotel.

But all the buildings
bordering these shores are
not devoted merely to ease
and pleasure, for as we return citywards, we pass a
number of huge flour mills,
which despite the fact that they
are industrial establishments are
still architecturally attractive, forming

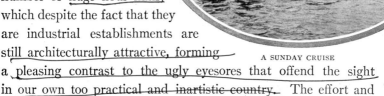

A SUNDAY CRUISE

a pleasing contrast to the ugly eyesores that offend the sight
in our own too practical and inartistic country. The effort and
outlay that tend to make sightly the temples of industry and

SALTSJÖBADEN

EXCELLENT ARCHITECTURE

commerce are not wasted.   Man does the better work the better his
surroundings.   The beautifying of factories should not be regarded
as a fad — it is a wise investment; beauty *is* an asset with a definite market value. Would the public
pay to see my pictures on the screen
if I showed them nothing but the
plain and practical? I have
found the trade in beauty fairly profitable, and I hope that
Mr. Pierpont Morgan will
some day realize the possi-
bilities of organizing beauty,
and proceed to form a gigantic Beauty Trust, and force
us all to join it for the everlasting benefit of the entire world.

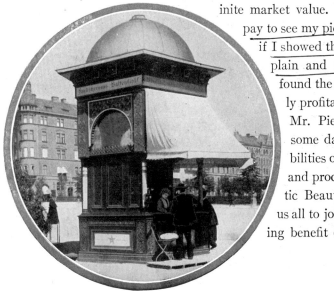

SOFT DRINKS

Thus dreaming of a future that will be beautiful even in the material and literal meaning of the word, we sail back to Stockholm, as thoroughly delighted with the suburbs as with the capital itself. In one thing, however, we are disappointed. We see so little in the way of characteristically Swedish dress. We had been several days in town before we saw a single

APARTMENTS

dress that could by any stretch of the imagination be regarded as a national costume. The women of the Swedish capital affect the styles and modes familiar in all the civilized communities of northern Europe. This was a bitter disillusion, for we, like many other sanguine travelers, had been lured to Sweden by the hope of seeing thousands of pretty girls in curious costumes, like those made so familiar by the colored photographs of Swedish beauties sold at all international expositions. We looked expectantly for such types, but when we found them in the streets, they were only in the bud, —sweet little Swedish ladies five or six years old. When we found them at sixteen or over, they were invariably serving as waitresses in gardens or cafés, togged out in Swedish costumes only for the hours of service, eager to get back into their ordinary clothes, and usually a trifle self-conscious and ill at ease in their extremely pleasing peasant

FOR THE STUDY OF BIOLOGY

dress. Surely they would not feel at home in the quaint old country cottages that we have seen in pictures. "Where must we go to find the old-time peasant life, to see the old-time dress, and study Swedish country costumes?" is the question that the traveler eventually asks after he has sought in vain to find

TWO LAPLAND
SPECIMENS

in Stockholm that which he seeks. The answer is invariably, "Why, in Skansen." Where and what is Skansen? Is it a village or a country district? Is it far from Stockholm? Must we take a train? Skansen is close at hand; we may go thither in a cab or ferry — it is both a village and a district, but it is primarily a museum, an open-air museum of Swedish life and costumes, an ethnographical exhibition intended to perpetuate the interesting things, the disappearance of which the modern traveler now deplores. Skansen is rural Sweden reproduced in the midst of a suburban park, seven thousand acres in extent. It is more than a reproduction, it is real sections of rural Sweden transplanted bodily from various remote regions to the capital. For everything we see at Skansen is real; the vehicles ranged near a cottage

THE "ÖL" GIRLS

once served the needs of sundry farmers many years ago; the
dwelling itself was once the home of some thrifty peasant family
in the heart of old-time Sweden. Let us enter it. We find the
table spread as if for a feast; the dishes and adornments are there
upon the cloth where they tell their own story, not as in ordinary

IN A PEASANT DWELLING AT SKANSEN

museums, shut up in glass cases and thus robbed of more than
half their interest and illustrative value. Do you not always
feel, when gazing at objects ranged stiffly in the sealed show-cases
of the average museum, that all those things are dead and almost
meaningless? Here, on the contrary, everything we see appears
to be related to the life of which it at one time formed a part;
even the simplest, rudest detail is eloquent of the reality, the
humanness of the vanished epoch that is depicted here. Eloquent,
too, of the God-fearing life led by the old-time peasantry is the
Klockstapel, the sharp steeple of the shingled tower of which the

THE "KLOCKSTAPEL" AT SKANSEN *bell tower*

bells were wont to call the country-side to prayer. Then there are ancient runic stones, medieval dwellings, and modern folk in quaint old costumes to dwell in them, and to dance the folk-dances and sing the folk-songs of Sweden round the May pole on the old festal days. Nowhere in the world is there a museum founded upon a more radical and rational idea. Our museums, with their cold, classified, and catalogued curiosities

HISTORIC STONES

IN AN OPEN AIR MUSEUM

ranged on monotonous shelves, are studied by the few and skimmed through or shunned by the many, but a museum such as Skansen, where the things that illustrate the art, history, religion, or domestic life or architecture of a nation are so displayed that they need no labels to explain them, is a museum to inspire

A TRANSPLANTED RURAL REGION

the student, and to delight and at the same time teach the multitude. Such a museum was planned for our own country — the method of grouping and display identical, but the scope far wider — not confined to one race or country, but expanded to embrace the entire world. The man who evolved the

OLD-TIME RURAL ARCHITECTURE
AT SKANSEN

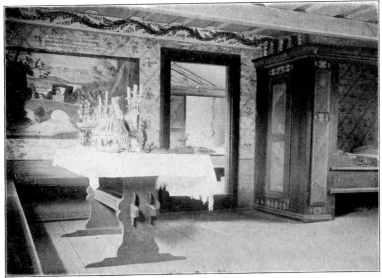

OLD–TIME ELEGANCE

splendid scheme of which I speak gave to it the greater part of a long, useful life. He pointed out the possibility of realizing his ambitious plan at a comparatively small cost; but he received little encouragement from a careless public and a very busy government. I speak of Mr. Franklin Webster Smith of Washington, perhaps best known to the American traveling public as the creator of the Pompeian houses in Washington and Saratoga, and as the builder of the Moorish villa Zorayda at St. Augustine. These structures, each a beautifully complete illustration of the domestic surroundings of artistic races, he gave to the world as suggestions, on a small scale, of what he hoped to see one day accomplished on a world-wide plane in a series of National Galleries at Washington, where, in successive terraced courts upon

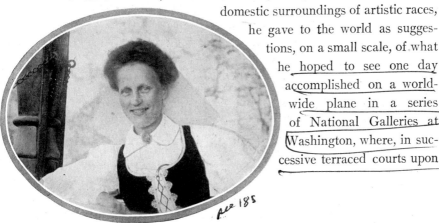

"LYCKLIG RESA!"

the slope of the old Observatory Hill, which would be crowned by a reproduction of the Parthenon — the world's most perfect structure — the visitor would find magnificently satisfying reproductions of all the most beautiful constructions of the world, from the Alhambra of Granada to the Nikko Temples of Japan, from the Assyrian palaces to the sanctuaries of Yucatan. The material

THE NORTHERN MUSEUM AND THE CITY FROM THE BREDABLICK

of which all these complex structures could be *cast*, not built, is concrete, — cheap, durable, and admirably adapted to the reproduction of the most ornate architectural forms.

Franklin Smith died before his magnificent and very practical plans received the attention that they merited. He had spent his private fortune in trying to prove, through artistic and costly object-lessons, the value and the practicability of those plans. It is, however, to be hoped that his labors and his dreams were not in vain and that some future day will witness a realization of his superb scheme in a series of National Galleries of Art and History and Architecture that will be to the world what Skansen is to Sweden.

From a look-out tower called the Bredablick at Skansen we see, as we gaze cityward, the huge buildings of the Northern Museum. That splendid institution is the outgrowth of the humble little ethnographic exhibition founded by the celebrated Dr. Artur Hazelius, who was also the creator of Skansen, which practically

HASSELBACKEN

is its outdoor annex. Hazelius too, like our own Franklin Smith, had to struggle with the apathy of legislators, press, and public, but he persisted and lived long enough to get results. At first, unaided, he gathered his modest collections, housing them in the upper rooms of cheap old buildings, admitting the public at a nominal fee, until at last the nation awoke to the value of his vast idea and gave him the means to further it, so that to-day, even in their present state of development, the Northern Museum and Skansen are among the most conspicuous institutions in all Sweden. Hazelius the elder died ere his work was half completed,

A COUNTRY BANGÅRD

but he left perfected plans, and his son, working now under government auspices, will ere long see the dream of his dead father
realized in full. The nation has taken to heart the words of
Artur Hazelius, who in pleading for his plans declared:
"The day will come when all our gold will not be enough to
buy an accurate picture of the times long past."

The proverb that "God made the country and man
made the town" holds good in Sweden, where both
the towns and the country are particularly well made.
There is nothing especially ornate about a Swedish
city; there is nothing frivolously pretty about the
Swedish landscape. Both town and country bear
the stamp of enduring worth and frank simplicity.
I have made the statement that Sweden is more like
the United States than any other of the European
countries. This demands a word of explanation. I
mean that in general outline the Swedish country-side
bears a remarkable similarity to many of the most
commonplace and prosperous regions in our eastern

TOURING

states.   We find the same indifferent roads, the same rail fences, telegraph poles, and railway crossings; the general aspect of the fields and farms is similar, and the rural architecture is not sufficiently unlike that of our own country to injure the illusion of a Scandinavian New England, or a Central New York Sweden,

THE REAL RURAL SWEDEN

save that the little Red School House crops out here too numerously, for the walls of nearly every farm house have usurped the warm tone which we associate with the outside of the country school.   Nor are school houses lacking in the country districts. Sweden believes in educating every citizen, and would look upon illiteracy as a national reproach.   Among the studies the English language receives a fair share of attention, and the frequency and fluency with which it is spoken makes the path of the Anglo-Saxon tourist indeed an easy one.   And even the older folk who did not learn it when at school will, when asked if they speak English, reply: "O, yas, I bin tree yar in Minnesota."

A COUNTRY CAMPANILE

Very interesting is a little journey that we make into Dalarne or Dalecarlia, the very heart of the Swedish fatherland, that we may see the old-time peasant costume actually worn and worked in, not merely donned for exhibition purposes as in Stockholm. At first we are intensely disappointed. We look in vain for bits of local color amid the folk assembled at the stations; they are all utterly beyond the pale of picturesqueness, arrayed in the habiliments of cosmopolitan conventionality. At last, however, at one wayside stop, we

IN DALARNE

sight a promising beginning, for there we positively discover two
Swedish caps and three striped Swedish aprons worn by women
who were waiting for the train. Still the costume is not complete; the women wear shirt-waists instead of the old-style
bodices, and the effect is spoiled. A little farther on we are

A DALECARLIAN VILLAGE

cheered by an architectural foretaste of better things, for as we
speed past a hillside village we spy a pointed steeple, properly
spired and shingled, in fact almost as picturesque as the one
on exhibition at Skansen in Stockholm. But similar rewards are
few and far between. Rural Sweden may be prosperous and admirable, its people virtuous and happy, but neither the land nor
the inhabitants thereof are calculated to arouse the ardor of the
traveler who seeks the grandiose in scenery, or the quaint and
curious in costumes and in customs.

But just as we have given up all hope of finding a real peasant
honestly wearing a real peasant dress, we are rebuked for our lack

NEAR RÄTTVIK

of faith by the sudden apparition of the long-sought Swedish maid in complete and satisfying Swedish costume with apron, cap, *and* bodice. But on beholding her we sit us down and laugh until we cry, for our old-fashioned maiden had come spinning down the hill upon a modern bicycle! Happily this does not rob us of our

A DALECARLIAN GÅRD

presence of mind, for ere the humor of the situation overwhelms us we press the button and secure a photographic proof that the Swedish peasant costume is still worn by at least one fair cyclist in the heart of Dalarne.

But seriously let me hasten to assure you that had we time to stop here over Sunday we

DALECARLIAN COSTUMES . . . AND
A BICYCLE

should then see perhaps a hundred handsome costumes worn by the wives and daughters of the rich farmers, who dwell in isolated farms around the fertile shores of the beautiful Lake Siljan. Every Sabbath day, long slender church-boats

DE SKÖNA FLICKÖRNA

come to town bringing
each a load of farmer folk
arrayed in special Sunday finery.   Then even the men deign
to assume their old-time dress, — a quaint, stiff, simple costume, of which we see on week days only an occasional
threadbare specimen, worn by working-men who are too
poor to modernize their week-day raiment,
and therefore forced to work in their old
Sunday-go-to-meeting togs.

Returning southward to the capital we soon set forth again to see
other aspects of provincial Sweden
in the island province of Gotland.
Embarking on a sea-going steamer,
we begin our voyage by threading
the salt-water channels that extend
eastward toward the open Baltic Sea,
some forty miles away.   As we already
know, Stockholm lies between two archipelagoes:
one set amid the lakes and the other in the salty
sound that stretches up and down the eastern

" PASS PÅ ! "

" DET LILLA BARNET "

coast of Sweden. Ten minutes after casting off the moorings, our steamer is gliding like a frightened swan along the channels that curve and wind amid the villa-dotted islands of the suburbs. The pilot must be keenly active to guide the skimming hull safely along the tortuous and deceptive channels. There seem to be

THE NEWEST THEATER

scores of them from which to choose at every turn, but without hesitation he brings us to what may be called one of the gates of Stockholm, the narrow pass between the town and fort of Vaxholm. There is no other entrance possible for deep-draught ships to the inner archipelago. By blocking this easily defended passage the Swedes could hold in check the navies of the world and prevent the bombardment of their capital. But even after having passed their forts we are not yet out of the wooded islands. Throughout the afternoon and far into the pale bright night, we glide along amid the million scraps of earth that go to form the famous Skärgård along this portion of the Swedish coast.

We steam past island after island; some low, barren, and deserted; some hilly, densely wooded, and inhabited by sturdy fisherfolk, who hasten to the rocks along the shore to wave a greeting and a farewell to the passing passengers. The Swedes are the most frantic wavers I have ever seen; upon the slight-

STOCKHOLM, THE V

est provocation, out come the snowy handkerchiefs, always so clean that we suspect that special ones are kept in special pockets exclusively for waving purposes. On station platforms and on steamboat piers we always see hundreds of fluttering handkerchiefs; these herald our approach long before we can discern the welcoming throng beneath them, and the same flock of white wings seems to hover there long after distance has made the wavers indistinguishable.

But weary of watching for the night which will not come at

all, we seek our bunks, while it is still bright enough to read on deck by the sunset glow of ten P. M., and on the following morning we wake in the harbor of the forgotten city which we have come so far to see. It is Visby on the west coast of the isle of Gotland, which lies in the open Baltic about midway between the Swedish

NORTH, BY NIGHT

coast and Russia. Leaving Stockholm in the afternoon the traveler reaches Visby the next morning at an early hour.

To speak of Visby eight hundred years ago was to name the richest city in this quarter of the globe. Even before the year 1200, Visby had attained renown as the Occidental terminus of the trading route along which Oriental merchandise was brought from the depths of Asia, by caravan, to Novgorod in Russia, and thence dispatched to the storehouses of Visby, whence it was distributed to the various markets of northwestern Europe.

THE SALTSJÖN

Visby's walls were built late in the thirteenth century, by which time Visby had become one of the chief towns of the Hanseatic League, that famous association of commercial towns formed for the protection of their trading ships from pirates, and the defense

LOOKING TOWARD THE DJURGÅRDEN

of their merchants from the rapacity of the old-time feudal princes, who were little better than aristocratic robbers.   To tell the story of the Hanse League would call for a long lecture upon a subject that is of intense interest not only because of its romantic and adventurous motive, but because of its practical influence upon the commercial conditions of to-day.   Modern commerce owes much of its security to the courageous old Hanse traders, who in com-

VAXHOLM

bining against the land-pirates and the thieves upon the sea, established the conditions that made possible the growth and increase of an international interchange of merchandise and pro-

ducts.   The men of Visby did their share of that good work, and their reward was more than proportionately great, as is attested by the splendor of the churches reared by them in thankfulness for their well-merited

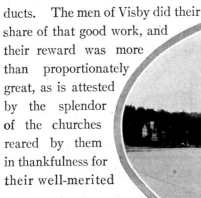

OFF FOR GOTLAND

prosperity. There were fourteen magnificent sanctuaries within
the city walls; three of them have disappeared, the others standing amid the modest homes of modern Visby like eleven skeletons
of a dead past, their colossal ancient shapes rising above the
little modern dwellings, like the whitened bones of the extinct
mammoth beside the forms of the ordinary creatures of to-day.

VASA'S CASTLE OF VAXHOLM

Eloquently do they tell of that far-off day of lavishness when the
men of Gotland — so the chroniclers inform us — were so rich
that they weighed their gold with twenty-pound weights and played
chess with jewels, while their pigs ate from silver salvers and their
women used golden distaffs in their spinning. To-day all this is
changed, and the inhabitants now refer sadly to their peat-bogs
as the only Gotland gold mines.

The confederation of Hanse towns has been sundered; three
of them only — Hamburg, Lübeck, and Bremen — retain their old
titles as Hanse towns, while Visby, isolated in the cheerless Baltic,
has been abandoned by the merchant fleets that once came eagerly

THE VISBY TOURIST BUREAU

into her profitable port. There were ninety cities in the league when it was at the height of its success and power. This was about the year 1280. Then as this corner of the world began to civilize itself, the need of the Hanse influence decreased and the confederation gradually declined until at the last recorded meeting of its representatives in 1669, only six towns sent deputies to attend what proved to be the obsequies of a venerable institution that had outlived its usefulness. But Visby's brief and far-off period of practical

A GOTLAND GIRL

ascendancy was not without its permanent result. There is no ship that sails the modern seas, unless she be a pirate craft, that does not trim her course commercially according to the maritime law of the civilized world which is founded upon the code of rules laid down by the wise mariners of Visby eight hundred years ago. The city has degenerated to a village, trim and quaint and pretty; a place of refuge for those weary of the world, and an ideal retreat for lovers on a honeymoon.

The Swedish tongue is spoken by the fifty thousand people who now inhabit Gotland, which is the largest island of the Baltic.

VISBY

But though Gotland is now a Swedish province it was the spoil of Denmark for many years after the assault of the city and the massacre of its inhabitants

WALLS AND TOWERS

THE RAMPARTS OF A FALLEN HANSE TOWN

by barbarous King Valdemar in the year 1361. A strange tale had its birth in that historical event; they tell us that a daughter of Visby, enamoured of the foreign king who came to plunder the city of her fathers, betrayed the town to him, and that her own people, in punishment, seized the

A GATE
WITHOUT
A SENTRY

traitorous maiden and built her body into the walls of a tower they were then repairing. It has ever since been called the Jungfrutorn — the Maiden's Tower. It would appear as if every walled city must have the fate of some unhappy maiden linked to its medieval towers. The maiden in the tower has mutely appealed to us for lo! these many centuries, and this particular one, the most unhappy of her class, certainly deserves our tardy tears, perhaps as well as any of the others.

SOME OF THE FORTY-EIGHT HIGH TOWERS NOW TENANTLESS

The story of how Gotland "got there" originally is a curious one. When the earth was young there floated freely in the Baltic wastes an island, which, though real, behaved very like a phantom. It never cruised by day. 'T was never visible except by night. Men saw

REMINDERS OF GOTLAND'S DAYS OF GLORY

it gliding o'er the waters when the moon was in the sky, but at
the ascent of the mystery-revealing sun the island sank, to rise
again only when the night shadows fell upon the waves. The
ancient mariners believed that could some brave man land upon
that elusive shore and light a fire there, the island would take

VISBY, A VILLAGE IN A CITY'S SHELL

root in the deep sea and end its wanderings forever. At last the
son of old King Guti, lord of the Jutland realm, driven by famine
from his father's land, was guided by a raven to the floating isle,
and, setting foot thereon with a small following, he kindled fires
to warm and cheer his crew, and the itinerant land at last stood
still. Tjällver,—that was his name,—remembering his father,
called the land Gutiland, and men call it Gotland to this day. So
rapidly did the population of the arrested wander-land increase
that at one time space lacked, and lots were cast to see which one
man of every three should leave the overcrowded isle. The

exiles went to Greece,—so say the chroniclers,—and their descendants dwell there even now.

Later, in near-historic times, men came from Pomerania to Gotland and founded Visby on its shores, calling their settlement Visby because it rose upon the site of an ancient "Vi," a place

HUMBLE HOMES AMID STATELY ECCLESIASTIC RUINS

of sacrifice. Other chroniclers insist that Visby was founded by a holy Amazon, whose bones were venerated in a Gotland church until the great Linnæus, coming to examine them, discovered that they were whale-bones! As this was before the days of tight-laced fashion we cannot suspect that the lady saint was buried in a C. B. à la Spirite shroud.

Counting the churches of Gotland, one may easily credit the statement that the island once had so many inhabitants that one in every three was crowded out. Not in Visby only, but in all the little towns and villages that stand so sleepily to-day on Gotland's

PICTURESQUE GOTLAND

shores, we find the church towers which in that prosperous yesterday rose "not single *spires* but in battalions." One may drive
around the island, which is seventy miles long and about thirty
wide, and almost never be out of sight of a church steeple. A
church-building mania at one time possessed all Gotlanders who

IN VISBY'S LANES

happened to be well-to-do.   In Visby stand the "Sister Churches,"
St. Drotten and St. Lars, side by side, built by two sisters, daughters
of a wealthy merchant, because they were jealous each of the
other — even in the days when Easter bonnets were unknown.
Astonishingly rich were all these churches, if the old tales are to be
believed.   In the rose windows of the grandest of them there
gleamed those famous gems — those carbuncles of painful name
and priceless worth, "the likes of which were not to be found in
the whole earth; they lighted the night as the sun does the day,
and greatly the people mourned their loss," for they, like all of
Visby's treasures, were carried off by the bad King Valdemar.
'T is said that they had even served as beacons for the ancient mariners, so brightly shone those high-set, luminous and lovely jewels.

THE CATHEDRAL OF ST. MARY, THE ONLY OLD CHURCH NOW IN USE

VISBY'S RUINED CHURCHES . . .

But little good had the Danish conqueror of all the wealth he took from Visby town. His treasure ship — loot-laden — foundered off a neighboring isle, and Visby's wealth lies there to-day, under the cliffs of Carlsö. 'T is said that when the day is

. . . HAVE GARDENS ON THEIR ROOFS

clear and the eye keen the ship itself is ofttimes seen far down
at the sea's bottom, the piles of plunder in her hold guarded by
a sable-coated dog of most ferocious mien. Not to be touched
is that treasure so sacrilegiously garnered by the wicked Valdemar and so justly rapt from his kingly clutches — at least, not
to be touched with any hope of recovery until there shall be born
twin calves which shall be reared on milk and never know the
taste of water. These shall some day drag the treasure from

ONE OF MANY MELROSE-LIKE RUINS

the deep. Superstitious Gotland farmers have actually reared
twin calves with the intent of trying out the truth of the old-
time belief. A volume could be compiled of the quaint superstitions of the people of this isolated province in the Baltic.
Olaf, the great Norwegian saint, came hither once upon a time

THE WALLS OF VISBY FROM THE ROOF-GARDEN OF A RUINED CHURCH

to save the people who in his day of course were heathen. A
heathen host, in battle array, opposed the Christian Norseman
and the militant missionary army that came with him. Olaf and
all his holy fighting men fell on their knees and prayed for
victory. Heaven vouchsafed the victory in answer to the prayer,
and Nature preserved a proof that the prayer was made, for the
marks of St. Olaf's knees are still to be seen on the rocky cliff-
top of the Gotland *klint*. The victorious but very practical
soldier of the cross granted quarter only to such of the pagan

natives as would receive baptism and deliver to him a goodly
golden ransom for their lives.

The poor Gotlanders have known all the ups and downs of
fortune. At one time the richest folk of northern Europe, there
came another time when as subjects of the Danish Queen Christina,
they and their land were actually pawned to Jacob Momma, a
Jewish money-lender, who squeezed a magnificent rate of interest
out of his island pledges.

Gotland suffered also from the "Spirits' Plague" in the days
when brandy making and the selling of it were the chief concern

A SYMBOL OF HANSEATIC POWER

of the government.
It is said that
one of the arch-
bishops warned
the King, saying,
"Sire, there are
two things a wise
King of Sweden
never meddles
with — religion
and brandy." But
it continued cus-
tomary for peas-
ants to purchase
liquor "by order
of the King,"
in order that the
royal treasury
might be kept
full — by keeping
the peasants also
in a like condition.
Then when the
royal distiller died,

IN MODERN VISBY

the monopoly died with him, but the national thirst he had cultivated, for economic reasons, lived on unquenched and apparently
unquenchable. All Swedes became amateur distillers for a time.
Brandy or *bränvin* — so says Horace Marryat, a writer of the

" TOOTING HIS TOOTER "

last century —became the coin of the realm;
horses and cattle were purchased and paid
for by measure of brandy; servants received it as payment in lieu of wages.
In 1840, when Marryat was first
touring Sweden, "each village on a
Sunday presented a fearful scene
of intoxication," but in 1862, so
great was the improvement, due to
the preaching of Canon Wieselgren of Gothenburg and to the
efforts of his followers, that "during a year's sojourn he never once
came across a drunken peasant."

But Blue Laws existed in Gotland
before the reform came. For example,
church-going was practically obligatory.
We are assured that "no man was allowed
to pass by a church during service time without

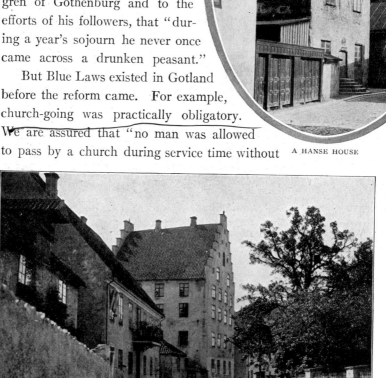

A HANSE HOUSE

DATING FROM THE DAYS OF THE LEAGUE

entering to hear the sermon!" It must have been a glorious age
for the preachers! In Visby church doors yawned for the unwary
Sunday stroller every hundred paces; there was nothing for it
but to emulate the door and join the yawners in the pews within.

THE RESTORED CATHEDRAL OF ST. MARY FROM THE MARKET

Visby churches are made of the sandstone for which the island
was well and favorably known to the architects of northern Europe.
The royal palaces of Stockholm, Copenhagen, Berlin, Dresden,
and St. Petersburg are built in part of stone taken from the Gotland quarries. Visby itself has been called "a quarry, feeding, as
it were, on her own vitals," for the houses of the present have
eaten much of the material of the walls and gates and towers of
the past.

The edges of the island present naked, quarry-like walls to

THE KLINT OR CLIFFS OF
GOTLAND

the winds of the blustery Baltic. The Swedish word for cliff is *klint*, and whiter than the famous cliffs of eastern Albion are the *klints* of Gotland's western coast. Straight from the sea they rise, gleaming and colorless, mirrored pale and ghostlike in the blue of the surrounding deep. Pure white, upright, calm, and commanding, they face the near but unseen motherland where dwell a race of men who give us the same impression that we get in looking at these cliffs. There is a rugged yet refined simplicity and dignity about the pale-haired Swedish Northmen that seems to make them kindred to these landmarks of their northern seas.

The Swedish people are to-day among the most admirable in Christendom. Enlightened, educated, with broad views of life, broad conceptions of the duty that every man owes

MIDSUMMER NIGHT

to civilization, the Swedes stand with other Scandinavians in the vanguard of the progress of the world. Scandinavia commands our admiration not so much because she has produced the greatest thinkers or the ablest men of action — and there is a noble list of names in the Scandinavian roll of honor — but because she has produced three honest nations, the Norwegians, Danes, and Swedes. The traveler in many other countries must be continually on the alert to foil the endless schemes for cheating or

THE ABANDONED BALTIC

robbing him; schemes practiced by hotel proprietors, servants, porters, shopkeepers, agents, cabmen, small boys, and beggars, but in Scandinavia he never for a moment questions the honesty of those with whom he comes in contact. He takes it for granted that he will be dealt with honestly. The simple unsuspiciousness of those with whom he deals allays in the breast of the oft-cheated Continental wanderer who reaches their hospitable shores all fear of double-dealing, and arouses in him a spirit of trustfulness that blesses both the stranger and the blond sons of Scandinavia, who by their innate honesty have restored to him his faith in human nature. If I were asked to speak in one brief sentence the eulogy of these northern nations that lie between the Baltic and the polar sea I should say simply this: "Here is the home of the honest men."

TOWARD FINLAND

FINLAND

ALTHOUGH Finland lies between Sweden and Russia, and although it has belonged to Sweden and now belongs to Russia, it is neither Swedish nor Russian. Nor is it a mere buffer state inhabited by a mixed population made up of mongrel communities, part Scandinavian and part Slavonic.

Finland is literally "Finn Land"—the land of the Finns. The Finlanders are a race apart, distinguished from their neighbors on the west and on the east by all the marks that make for separate nationality. In appearance they are unlike the Swedes

LAND'S END AT HANGÖ

and unlike the Russians. They have the high cheek bones and the slant eyes of their cousins in the Asiatic Orient, for they are closer kin to the Japanese than to the Swedes. The Magyars of Hungary are of their race; and the Mohammedan Turks are nearer to them ethnologically than the orthodox Russians. The Tatars, scattered in various parts of Russia and Siberia, blazed the trail by which the Oriental fathers of the Occidental Finns made their way across the wilderness of two continents in days so remote that no man may say just when these aliens from the East came to make a little nation for themselves up almost in the extreme northwest corner of the continent of Europe.

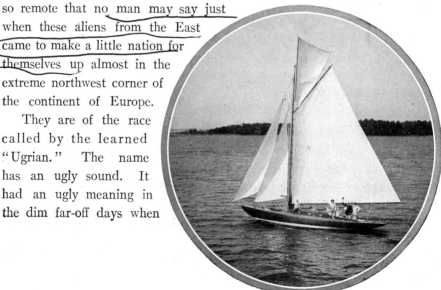

They are of the race called by the learned "Ugrian." The name has an ugly sound. It had an ugly meaning in the dim far-off days when

IN A FINNISH FJORD

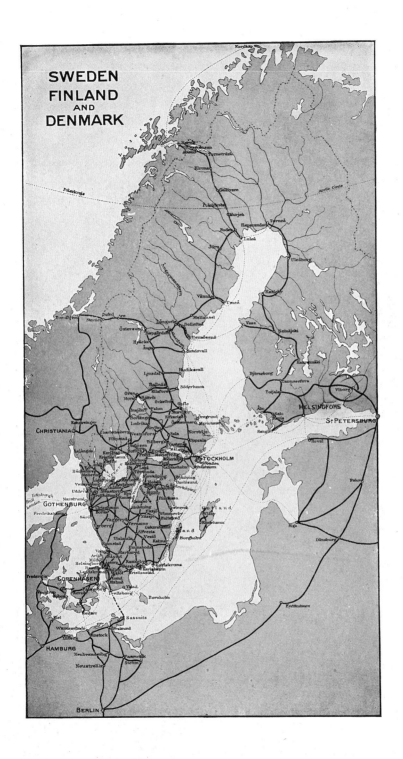

the Ugrian hordes swept like a barbaric devastating flood over the civilized lands that lay in their westward path. Mothers and nurses in those days quieted naughty children with the menace that the Ugrian would get them, and in the Ugrian of the

ENTERING HELSINGFORS HARBOR

medieval child we recognize the "Ogre" of our childish fears and superstitions. But the Finnish ogre, having found a happy habitat, has become in the course of cen-turies a cultivated gentleman. We meet him without fear; in fact, we are delighted to mingle with him and his domesticated fellows on the ship that bears us to the shores of the land that he has made his own.

As a rule he speaks our language — several languages, for his own is known only to

THE SWEDISH CAPTAIN OF THE
" DÖBELN "

FINNISH FAREWELLS

himself. The Finnish language is said to be a branch of the Oriental Finno-Ugric tongue, of which the Hungarian language is another branch. The Lapps who dwell in Swedish and in Norwegian Lapland speak a Finnish dialect. Those little brown people whom we met near the North Cape are related even to the Mongols and the Manchus who dwell on the farthest eastern edge of the hemisphere. So much the scientist affirms. But the traveler is inclined to extend the boundary of family and make the Finns kin to the

ON THE QUAY AT HELSINGFORS

Kanakas of Hawaii, when he reads upon the map of Finland
place-names as soft and liquid as the names of places in the
Paradise of the Pacific. When we pronounce names like Puu-
mala, Punkaharju, Sulkava, Kuopio, Kajana, Kalavesi and Uleå
we seem to see the Hawaiian palm-trees waving at Honolulu, the

THE FISH MARKET AT HELSINGFORS

sugar cane ripening on Maui, or the blue surf breaking on the
rocks at Punaloo or on the beach at Waikiki.

Though not an island, Finland is a land of countless islands.
The interior is like a landlocked archipelago, high above sea
level, and — amazing statement — going higher every year. All
Finland is rising bodily out of the Baltic. Towns which were
little seaports two hundred years ago, are now inland villages
three miles from the shore. The wreckage of old ships is now and

then plowed up by the farmers who till the inland farms. This
uplift is most rapid in the north, where the land rises at a rate of
several feet a century. Even in the south, within the memory
of man, islands have become united with the mainland and now
pose as peninsulas. Finland is well called "The Last-born

FINNISH FISHERFOLK

Daughter of the Sea." She is being slowly lifted out of the sea's
embrace by what might be designated a "land wave," that now
swells from north to south. Naturally enough, at the same time
and at about the same rate, the land that lies on the southern
shore of the Gulf of Finland is sinking. The sea is consoling itself
for the loss of Finland by possessing itself of little strips of territory
along the edges of the Baltic provinces of Russia. In winter even
the waters of the sea become like unto land. The icy touch of

the arctic winter transforms even the salty Gulf of Bothnia into a frozen desert, across which men may make their way in sledges from a point just north of Åbo, the old capital of Finland and now a town of 46,000 prosperous souls, to the neighboring Swedish coast, about a hundred miles away.　　There is a regular international　　　　　　　　　　　　　　　　post-road of　　　　　　　　　　　　　　　　　　　　　　　　　　ice

THE MARKET SQUARE OF HELSINGFORS

from shore to shore, and it is called "The Winter Way."　Silent and terrible must be that ephemeral but annually reappearing province of ice, traversed by that Great White Way that forms the winter sledge route between those northern lands.

　　The first we see of Finland, coming by steamer from Stockholm in the summer season, is the Port of Hangö, a kind of land's end in the Baltic, to which, however, trains may come from Vladivostok on the Sea of Japan over one unbroken line of Russian railway nearly six thousand miles in length.　Thus are the Finns,

MUNICIPAL HOUSECLEANING

after long centuries of separation, brought near again to their forgotten kindred in the Orient. Japan and China, once distant
many months, are now less than eleven days away. From Hangö
we cruise along through landlocked lovely fjords amid ten thousand islands to Helsingfors, the
capital of Finland and now the
most populous of Finnish cities.
We come in a neat and trim
little Swedish steamer, which
makes the run from Stockholm
to St. Petersburg in about forty
hours, . touching *en route* at
Hangö, Helsingfors, and sometimes at Cronstadt, the
island fortress that
commands the
sea route
leading to
the Russian

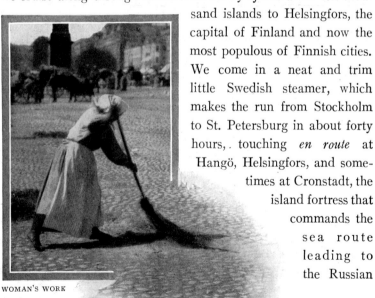

WOMAN'S WORK

ALMOST AMERICAN IN ASPECT

capital that Peter built upon the marshes of the Neva. Two hundred years ago there were six hundred souls in Helsingfors. To-day the population numbers one hundred and twenty-five thousand. It has been the capital only since the year 1812 when Russia, having taken Finland from the Swedes, removed the seat of government from the old capital of Åbo, which lay too far from St. Petersburg and too near to Sweden. Taking a leaf from the book of Peter the Great, the Tsar Alexander I had Helsingfors built to order, chiefly by the German architect Karl Ludwig Engel, who, laboring for a score of years, from 1820 until his death in 1840, created the superb "fiat" city that we see to-day. Much, of course, has been done since his time, but Helsingfors is none the less his creation. He gave it shape and form, endowed it with its most important buildings, and the city as we see it now might almost bear the name of Engelborg or Engel's

THE ESPLANADE

FINLAND'S POET RUNEBERG

city. It is almost American in aspect, were it not for the women working in the street. Finland has granted suffrage to women. There are nineteen "lady members" in the Finnish Diet, but there are more than nineteen of their sisters wielding the brooms of "white wings" in the broad clean streets of

BRÄN-VINS-BORD

the capital of the Grand Duchy. It may be well to remember that Finland is not a Russian province; it is not subject to the Tsar of All the Russias in his capacity as Tsar, though it is ruled by him as Grand Duke of Finland.

Judging from all accounts, the Finns at the time of the annexation

IN A HELSINGFORS RESTAURANT

of Finland to Russia were even anxious to obtain the protection of Russia, through the overlordship of the Tsar, for Sweden had not been too good to them in the days of her long domination.

Finland was not won by conquest. Russia had been frequently at war, not

SMÖRGÅSBORD

with the Finns, but the Swedes, trying to drive them from Finnish territory. During the Napoleonic wars, in 1808, the Russians came over the line again in force. The fortress of Sveaborg, near Helsingfors, was surrendered by the Swedish commander. A few Finns fought bravely in the north for the cause of their old masters, but meantime the Tsar Alexander I appealed squarely to the people of the land, offering

THE
LUTHERAN
CHURCH OF
ST. NICHOLAS

THE SENATE SQUARE

them independence in so far as Sweden was concerned, and the protection, not the tyranny, of Russia. An Act of Union was signed by a hastily convoked Finnish parliament. The Tsar became Grand Duke of Finland in 1809. The parliament did not meet again for fifty-four years, until convoked by his

MEMORIAL TO ALEXANDER II, TSAR OF ALL THE RUSSIAS, AND GRAND DUKE OF FINLAND

nephew, Alexander II, in 1863. Meantime the land was justly ruled, not as a province of autocratic Russia, but as a constitutional monarchy whose Grand Ducal rulers were fair-minded Tsars. Faithfully for a time did Russia keep the pledge contained in this declaration delivered to the Finns by the first Alexander, and to which they look as to a kind of Magna Charta. "Providence having placed us in possession of the Grand Duchy of Finland, we have desired, by the present act, to confirm

THE MEMORIAL CHURCH IN ST. PETERSBURG MARKING THE SITE OF THE ASSASSINATION OF ALEXAN-
DER II IN 1881. THE SECTION OF THE PAVED QUAY ON WHICH THE LIBERATOR FELL IS EMBRACED
BY THE CHURCH, PART OF WHICH EXTENDS OVER THE OLD BED OF THE CANAL IN ORDER TO
BRING THE ACTUAL SITE OF THE TRAGEDY WITHIN THE SANCTUARY.

*like St Basils
in Moscow?*

and ratify the religion and fundamental laws of the land, as well as the privileges and rights which each class of the said Grand Duchy in particular, and all the inhabitants in general, be their position high or low, have hitherto enjoyed according to the constitution. We promise to maintain all these benefits and laws firm and unshaken in their full force."

But in 1898 there comes a change in the fair policy of Russia toward the one free and really progressive part of her great empire. Nicholas II. attempts to alter the military law. He proposes to increase the Finnish army and the period of service, and to force the Finns to serve outside of Finland even in time of peace, which had not been done before his time. He issued an arbitrary ukase to the effect that all questions common to the whole empire should be decided

ALEXIS, TSAREVITCH OF ALL THE RUSSIAS AND FUTURE GRAND DUKE OF FINLAND, BORN 1904

in St. Petersburg by the Tsar and his advisers, thus making the Finnish Diet a mere Duma. Finland went into mourning; her postal authorities even issued jet-black postage stamps, and used them until the Russian post-offices were ordered to destroy all letters bearing that appealing little badge of mourning. Then

SWEARING ALLEGIANCE TO THE TSAR

the Finns put their black stamps inside the letters they were sending to the friends in Russia, every letter a protest against irresistible Russian political aggression. During these dark years emigration increased five-fold, for all who could escape from the land over which the awful Bobrikoff had been sent to tyrannize fled to the land of liberty over the ocean. At last, in 1904, the tyrant met his fate at the hand of a patriotic Finn almost at the threshold of the outraged national

MOHAMMEDAN CONSCRIPTS TAKING OATH IN PRESENCE OF A MULLAH OF THEIR FAITH

Senate. Russia heeded the warning
and adopted wiser policies, insist-
ing no longer on her hated
military laws. Finns need
not serve as Russian sol-
diers; Finland is now
allowed to make a cash
contribution toward the
national defense; the Finnish army has been dis-
banded, and on our last
visit to Helsingfors we
looked in vain for the clean,
trim, native soldiers whom we
had so admired several years before
when we first came to Finland. Instead
we saw — offensively numerous — the

A PRIEST OF THE ORTHODOX
FAITH

KISSING THE ICON OF THE ORTHODOX GREEK CHURCH

sturdy, dirty, swag-
gering Cossack, or the
smelly and imposing
looking Russian sol-
dier everywhere in
evidence.

The people of this
little nation, which
insists upon remain-
ing a nation and re-
sists so stubbornly all
attempts to merge it
with the polygenous
empire of the Ro-
manoffs, call them-
selves not Finns, but
Suomi. They have

their ancient literature; they have their epic poem — the Kale-vala, which means "Land of Heroes." It is one of the most delightfully readable of epics, translated admirably by an American scholar, Mr. J. M. Crawford, who was at one time our consul in St. Petersburg. Like the Greek epics, this one came not from the mind of one man, but from the hearts and lips of many; and

THE REGIMENT IN REVIEW

it has come down to us, not written on cold, stiff parchment, but inscribed in the warm hearts and phrased by the mobile lips of successive gen-erations of Runo-singers, the Suomi bards who sang the stories of their race as Homer and his fellow-singers sang the glories of the Greeks.

RUSSIAN OFFICERS

RUSSIAN CAVALRY

The Kalevala, which is seven thousand lines longer than the
Iliad, according to its own hauntingly lovely lines, is

"Filled with old-time incantations,
  Filled with songs of times primeval,
  Filled with ancient wit and wisdom;
  Sings the very oldest folk-songs,
  Sings the origin of witchcraft,
  Sings of earth and its beginning,
  Sings the first of all creations,
  Sings the source of good and evil,
  Sung, alas! by youth no longer."

SINGING AS THEY RIDE

FORMER DEFENDERS OF
FINLAND

"This is Hiawatha-like!" we murmur, but remember this was written long centuries before the land of Hiawatha was discovered. Longfellow first found his Hiawatha meter in a German translation of the Kalevala. The original is unrhymed, but it contains that more effective "rhyme of the sense," and that memory-aiding "rhyme of reiteration" that made it sink the deeper into the hearts and minds of those whose mission was to sing it to one generation and teach it to the next, that its unwritten beauties be not lost. Full of practical advice as well as beauty is this wondrous and to us almost unknown poem. Here is the counsel given to

OF THE DISBANDED FINNISH ARMY

IN RURAL FINLAND

the husband of the ancient days in case the wife whom he has chosen prove less acquiescent and obedient than a wife should be:

"Teach one year in words of kindness,
Teach with eyes of love a second,
In the third year teach with firmness.
If she should not heed thy teaching,

.   .   .   .   .   .

Then instruct her with the willow,
Use the birch-rod from the mountain,
In the closet of thy dwelling,
In the attic of thy mansion;
Strike her not upon the common,
Do not conquer her in public,
Lest the villagers should see thee,
Lest the neighbors hear her weeping."

THE NEW HOTEL AT IMATRA

Words of wisdom are addressed to all posterity by the Finnish Runo-singer through the mouth of the old enchanter who, with the accent of a prophet-sage, thus adjures the nations that are yet to wax and wane in the course of the unrolling centuries:

THE HARBOR OF HELSINGFORS

"Oh, ye many unborn nations,
    Never evil nurse your children,
    Never give them out to strangers,
    Never trust them to the foolish!
    If the child be not well nurtured,
    Is not rocked and led uprightly,
    Though he grow to years of manhood,
    Bear a strong and shapely body,
    He will never know discretion,
    Never eat the bread of honor,
    Never drink the cup of wisdom."

There are modern poets, too, in Finland. First among them in the hearts of his fellow-countrymen is Rune-berg, whose statue, moulded by his sculp-

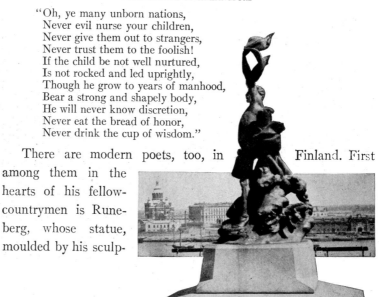

THE "SHIPWRECK"

A FINNISH PASTORAL

tor-son, adorns the Esplanade in Helsingfors. Painting and sculpture have
their Finnish servants, who serve
their mistress, Art, with a noble
faithfulness and a talent that is
in many cases akin to genius.

Nature, too, has showered
beauty-gifts on Finland. In
the north lies a region of
island-dotted lakes that is almost

THE CHUTES OF IMATRA

Japanese in its quaint loveli-
ness. At Imatra beauty
greets us in far
grander form, for
there Finland's
greatest cataract
thunders down
from calm Lake
Saima toward the
larger Russian lake, La-
doga, whose waters reach the
Baltic through the broad channel

CRUISING

of the Neva that flows beneath the many bridges of St. Petersburg. The falls of Imatra are rapids rather than cataracts;
the waters rage through a wild, rocky cut one third of a mile
long, dropping some sixty feet within that space. The lake region
above, which has been likened to a "milky way of islands," is
about two hundred and fifty feet above sea level, and has been

EVENING IN THE ARCHIPELAGO

made accessible by a canal, with twenty-eight locks, built by the
famous Ericsson in 1856.

Exquisite are the northern nights in Finland.   Some one has
said that "midnight is only a milder, gentler noon," for the sun
barely dips below earth's northern rim.   We saw a glorious sun
hanging like a harvest moon above Lake Saima long after the

THE SUN NEAR MIDNIGHT ON LAKE SAIMA

hour when suns of other lands have left the real moon to take
care of trysting lovers.

One very curious feature of the lake region in this northern
land is in the form of highroads that run right across the lakes!
There are so many islands and so many conveniently placed, long,
meandering peninsulas that but little difficulty has been encountered in extending the post-roads almost straight away over the
lakes.   Causeways have been constructed from isle to isle and
from peninsula to peninsula, using the intervening islands as
stepping-stones in the path that leads overland between the waters
of the myriad lakes and their communicating channels.   One
may thus enjoy in Finland the practically unique experience of

ÅBO CASTLE

cruising in an archipelago *by carriage!* Descending from the
watery highlands, we make our way by rail to Viborg, a seaport
on one of the narrow fjords of the Baltic, and very near to the

THE OLD ROUND TOWER CALLED "FAT KATERINA"

THE OLD CASTLE AT VIBORG

boundary line that is the only barrier between the Grand Duchy of Finland and the Russian Empire. At Viborg we begin to realize how near we are to Russia, for at Viborg we find not only the Russian soldier, but the Russian cabby and the Russian *droski*, and everywhere our eyes are vexed by those familiar and yet undecipherable Russian signs. The builders of Babel would feel at home in a compartment of a Finnish railway train — for there they would find warnings not to

THE VIBORG WATER-FRONT

put their heads out of the windows, in six different languages — Finnish, Swedish, Russian, French, German, and English. In Viborg there is an old castle that was founded in 1293 and taken by Peter the Great in 1710. A detached round tower near the water-front is known as the Fat Katerina, but whether or not it was named in honor of Catherine the Great we cannot say. Viborg was Russiafied a hundred years before the rest of Finland fell into Russian hands. It is now distant only four hours by rail from the capital of the Tsars, and the region round about is dotted with the summer homes of Petersburgers. Russia would like to possess all of Scandinavia,

VIBORG IS FAMOUS FOR ITS BREAD AND "KRINGLAS"

DROSHKY-LIKE DRAYS

MODERN VIBORG   *Russian border*

and were the Russian to take what he desires, it would be only to
repossess himself of his Fatherland, for the Russian Empire was
the creation of the Scandinavian adventurer, the Norseman Rurik.
Muscovy was founded by a Viking rover. Russia is but a colony of Scandinavians, grown greater than the homeland whence
they came; and yet how different the descendants of those who
stayed at home from those
who followed Rurik to the
Moskva and the Volga!
On the Russian side of

THE RUSSIAN
ISTVOSTCHIK . . .

. . . AND THE FINNISH CABBY

Russian side of

the line, autocracy, bureaucracy, popular ignorance, superstition, and tyranny; on the Scandinavian side, constitutional government, woman suffrage, universal education, religious freedom, and democratic liberty. In Russia *seventy-nine per cent* of the population is illiterate; in Scandinavia, illiteracy is practically non-existent.

Finland is the one really civilized corner of the empire of the Tsar, and if the autocrat of the Winter Palace were not blind he would cease trying to Russiafy Finland, and bend his every energy to the *Finnishing* of Russia that his great empire might rival, in the intelligence of its people and in the progressive spirit of its government, the Scandinavian lands whence came the men who founded Muscovy and made possible the career of Peter and the creation of St. Petersburg.

7/16/97

A SOLDIER OF THE TSAR

THE CATHEDRAL OF ROSKILDE

Until the year of our Lord fourteen hundred and forty-three the city of Roskilde was the capital of Denmark. It held at one time a population of one hundred thousand; today only about ten thousand dwell under the shadow of this thirteenth-century Cathedral, within which are the tombs of many Danish kings and queens. The name of Roskilde is dear to the heart of every loyal Dane, dearer even than the name of the new capital, Copenhagen, which lifts its towers and spires twenty miles away.

THE CATHEDRAL OF ROSKILDE

Until the year of our Lord fourteen hundred and forty-three the city of Roskilde was the capital of Denmark. It held at one time a population of one hundred thousand; today only about ten thousand dwell under the shadow of this thirteenth-century Cathedral, within which are the tombs of many Danish kings and queens. The name of Roskilde is dear to the heart of every loyal Dane, dearer even than the name of the new capital, Copenhagen, which lifts its towers and spires twenty miles away.

DENMARK

259

Denmark

GO around the world on any given parallel of latitude and you will find the lands through which you travel, broadly speaking, very much alike.

Go up and down the world on a meridian of longitude and you will note wide differences in every hundred miles. Travel through Portugal, Spain, southern France, Italy, Greece, and even Turkey, and at each new frontier you will see something to recall the lands that you have left behind. But travel northwards from Gibraltar toward the North Cape, and as each short degree of latitude is crossed the landscape changes color, and the faces fade until the rich brown or olive of Iberia gives place to the pale pink or sandy blond of Scandinavia.

The first time I came to Denmark I came almost directly from the sunny valleys of Braganza — saying *adeus* to the Portuguese, *bon jour* and *au revoir* to the Frenchmen of the south and north of France, and "Good morning" and "Good bye" to British cousins, to greet with a new, unfamiliar greeting the sturdy sons of Scandinavia, whose fathers were the predecessors of the Portuguese in maritime discovery and conquest by more than half a thousand years.

While Portugal was still in the possession of the Moors, the Danes were ruling half of England, parts of Ireland, Scotland, and of Normandy, and they had even threatened countries farther south. Six hundred years before the mariners of Portugal had crossed the south Atlantic or found the way to India the Scandinavian rovers had found and settled Iceland, and even touched the shores of North America.

HIS MAJESTY FREDERIK VIII, KING OF DENMARK

1906-12

Therefore, although we shall find in Denmark no reminders of the sunny Lusitanian land from which the Portuguese sea rovers set forth on their epic quests, we shall still find a people who of old were kindred to the heroes of the south in courage and in deeds of daring done upon the seas.

The reigning King of Denmark is his Majesty Frederik VIII, son of the late King Christian IX, who died in 1906. The royal consort of King Frederik is Queen Lowisa, daughter of King Charles XV of Sweden and Norway. The royal pair have seven children; the eldest son, Prince Christian, born in 1870, being of course heir apparent to the Danish throne, while the second son, Prince Karl, born in 1872, already has a throne of his own, for he was elected King of Norway under the title of Haakon VII in November, 1905. The invaluable Statesman's Year Book tells us that the crown of Denmark has been elective from earliest times; that the direct male line of the House of Oldenburg became

HER MAJESTY THE QUEEN OF DENMARK

[handwritten note: looked like Queen Mary of UK]

[handwritten margin notes: 1906–12 / 1863–1906 (88) / Christian X 1912–47]

extinct on the death of Frederik VII in 1863. In view of the death of the King without direct heirs, the Great Powers of Europe, "taking into consideration that the maintenance of the integrity of the Danish monarchy, as connected with the general interests of the balance of power in Europe, is of high importance

THE DEAD ROYALTY OF DENMARK

to the preservation of peace," had signed a treaty at London in 1852, by the terms of which the succession to the crown of Denmark was made over to Prince Christian of Schleswig-Holstein-Sonderburg-Glücksburg, who in due time became Christian IX of Denmark, "Grandfather of European royalty." Think of all the royal folk descended from that fine old man. Queen Alexandra of England and the Empress Dowager of Russia are his daughters; his eldest son is now on the Danish throne, and his second son is King George of Greece. One of his grandsons

THE LATE KING CHRISTIAN IX
OF DENMARK

is now ruling Norway as Haakon VII. The Czar of All the Russias and the King of England are sons of Christian's daughters, and his blood is in the veins of half the royal families of Europe. He died in 1906, at the age of eighty-eight, and in the forty-third year of his long reign. No monarch in the world was ever more respected, none more worthy of respect. "A good King of a good people" describes King Christian and his Danish subjects. Until his accession in 1863, King Christian was only a captain in the guards, as poor as any other Danish officer. He lived quietly in Copenhagen in the Amalia Street. It is even said that his wife and daughters did their own housework — and those daughters, then in their teens, have since graced the thrones of England and of Russia.

The present constitution of Denmark dates from 1849. There is a Danish Diet, called the Rigsdag, composed of two houses: the Landsthing or Senate, and the Folkething or House of Commons. Every male citizen who has reached his thirtieth year enjoys the franchise — for Danes are not "old enough to vote" until they are nine years older than the young Americans of voting age.

Denmark is one of the smallest states of Europe, smaller even

than Switzerland, but still occupying more space on the map than
Belgium or Holland. There is, however, practically no waste
land. The population of about two million six hundred thousand is spread very evenly over all parts of Denmark, with an
average density of one hundred and sixty-seven inhabitants to
the square mile. In Norway there are only eighteen human beings
to the square mile. Denmark, in contrast to her sister kingdom
across the Skager-Rack, is like a well-peopled and productive
paradise, finished and cared for like a park by a population
that covers or cultivates every available acre.

We embark for our little voyage to Denmark at Kiel, the great
naval port of Germany. The famous harbor of Kiel, the best
harbor of the Baltic, belonged to Denmark until the duchies of
Schleswig-Holstein were taken over by the Germans after the
war of 1864. Kiel gives its name to the great Prussian canal
that joins the North Sea and the   Baltic,
and thus cuts off what was
once the Continental part
of Denmark from the
mainland. As our sturdy
Danish steamer sweeps
down the magnificent
harbor, we note on
the shore the splendid
steel and glass sheds
for ship-building, and
moored in the channel
a number of German war-
ships, eloquent evidences
of Teutonic ascendan-
cy in Baltic waters.
From Kiel we come
to Korsör, a voyage of
about five hours across

A DANISH DAMSEL

the so-called "belts" or channels that lie between the mainland and Danish islands.   Korsör, the port at which we disembark, is situated on the western side of the island of Zealand.   To reach Copenhagen we must traverse the island at its widest part, traveling seventy miles by rail.

Denmark is literally an island kingdom, for even Jutland, which was originally and is still nomi-

LOOKING TOWARD THE THORVALDSEN MUSEUM

nally a pen- insula, has been made an island by the cutting of the Kiel Canal.   To enumerate all the islands proper would be to make a catalogue of titles almost impossible to pronounce properly.   Among these islands of the Danish archipelago the more important are Fünen, Laaland, Falster, Langeland, Möen, Bornholm, and Sjælland, the last known to the English-speaking world as Zealand.

The foreign possessions of Denmark are also chiefly islands: Iceland; the Faroe Islands; the West Indian Islands of St. Croix,

St. Thomas, and St. John, and the huge, seemingly useless snow-buried island called Greenland, which was discovered by the Norsemen a thousand years ago and given its alluring name, "Greenland," suggestive of sunshine and productivity, by Eric the Red, in order to lure settlers to a land to which no sane man would dream of going save in the course of a polar quest.

THE RAADHUS PLADS

Copenhagen is thus the capital of an island kingdom, the many parts of which are scattered far and wide over the face of the waters.

We find the Danish metropolis surprisingly attractive. We are amazed at many things,—the broad fine avenues, the modern buildings. We are delighted by the excellence of the hotel, from the windows of which we look out upon the Raadhus Plads and the new City Hall, a structure recently completed. Electric cars of twentieth-century design, noiseless and far more elegant than

those in many of our cities, glide across the square with almost
American celerity. There is an up-to-dateness about nearly
everything. For example, the elevators in the new Raadhus are
not only up to date, they are, as Clyde Fitch cleverly remarked
about one of his plays, "up to day after to-morrow." Approaching the "lifts" we find instead of one closed door two

THE NEW CITY HALL

open ones. There is no electric button for the waiting passenger
to push. It would be useless, for the passenger is not obliged to
wait; if he desires to go up, he merely steps through the portal
on the left, onto one of the open shelves which come gliding slowly
up that shaft in regular succession every fifteen seconds, and if
he wishes to descend, he steps through the right-hand portal, timing
his entrance to coincide with the passing of another open elevator
downward bound. There is a chain of twelve cars, like a vertical
moving sidewalk, operated by an electric mechanism. We made

several round trips; stepping aboard one of those open-front elevators we are carried to the uppermost story, then swung sideways to the other parallel shaft, down which our car glides slowly to the basement, there to be swung back to the shaft through which we first ascended. There are no attendants visible. The chance of accident is rendered small by the slow speed and by the fact that the thresholds of both the doorways and the cars are hinged, and would yield to pressure and release the careless foot

A DECORATIVE TROLLEY POLE

that might otherwise be caught and crushed. Up to date also are the amusement enterprises of the city. Not far from the new Raadhus is the famous pleasure park of Copenhagen, the Tivoli Garden, a sort of permanent World's Fair in miniature, and one of the oldest and most celebrated places of the kind in Europe. In addition to the great concert hall, with its Turkish domes and minarets, where a symphony orchestra plays every day, there are theaters and arenas, stages for acrobatics and for the pantomimes which have delighted Danish children for half a century; and there are temporary exhibitions of all varieties, and half a dozen excellent restaurants. Pictures

ARTISTIC ELECTRIC LIGHTING

THE GATE TO TIVOLI

made by day show the Tivoli deserted. At night, however, as many as fourteen thousand people are sometimes found within the gates, and every place of entertainment is then filled to overflowing. While dining there one evening we were introduced to several Danish journalists, who, learning of our object in coming to their city, proceeded to make things interesting for us on the following day by getting out the fire brigade for an exhibition run past our motion-picture cameras.

It may not be widely known, but it is a fact that

A TIVOLI FLOWER MAIDEN

Copenhagen possesses some of the finest museums and art galleries in Europe. The New Glyptothek contains a collection of modern statues that ranks high among the great collections of the world; in fact, modern

THE COPENHAGEN FIRE DEPARTMENT

French sculpture is nowhere, outside of France, so well represented as in this collection formed by Carl Jacobsen, a rich citizen, whose wealth, vast though it be, is more than equalled by his public spirit. He housed his won-derful

GIVING US AN EXHIBITION RUN

array of modern marbles in that splendid gallery, and gave the whole completed masterpiece, filled with masterpieces, to the State. "Let us labor for the Fatherland," is the motto of Carl Jacobsen.

TIVOLI TABLES

We read that motto above the monumental entrance to the famous Ny-Carlsberg Brewery, whence he derives the wealth that he is spending — for he is still spending. His collections he still deems incomplete, his galleries still too small to house the

A TIVOLI PALACE

treasures he intends to gather for the enjoyment and instruction of his fellow-citizens and of posterity. The New Glyptothek does not represent the half of his benefactions to the cause of art. There is also the Old Glyp-

tothek adjoining the Ny-Carlsberg Brewery which is less elegant externally, perhaps, but far more valuable than the museum in the city proper. It contains a collection of original Greek marbles and a series of Roman

THE ART MUSEUM

portrait-busts and statues which connoisseurs regard as the most precious and extensive collection of the kind, not only in northern Europe, but in the entire world. From the open windows of the halls where Roman Emperors, Greek sages, and classic gods and goddesses are assembled as in some mighty congress of

IN THE GLYPTOTHEK

the glorious artistic past, we may look out upon the courts of the adjacent brewery, listen to the rumble of the heavy keg-laden wagons, and breathe an atmosphere thick with the smell of hops and malt. But from another of these halls, likewise frequented by the marble shades of imperial Romans, intel-lectual Greeks, and superb sculptured creatures whom we

THE NEW GLYPTOTHEK

willingly call deities — because they are divinely beautiful — the privileged visitor may step into the private drawing-room of the collector Jacobsen, whose home is practically under the same roof. How admirable is this realized dream of the Copenhagen brewer! He enjoys all the pleasures of intimate possession, and yet his joy cannot be tainted by the thought that in gathering these things at fabulous expense he is merely pandering to selfish-ness. In giving all his treasures to the State while he is still alive, he has found the only way of entering into true possession of them. The man who has heaped up undue riches, if he have a sense of justice, must be haunted by the thought that he is not their rightful owner; that to possess them truly, to make good his spiritual title

SOME OF CARL JACOBSEN'S TREASURES

to them, he must be prepared to give them up. Above the entrance
to his home we read, in letters of mosaic, the words, "*Bien faire et
laissez dire*" — "Do your work well — and let 'em talk"; which

THE ROMAN PORTRAIT-BUSTS

THE GREEK MARBLES

recalls the gentle admonition with which our own Elbert Hubbard gently closes his preachments, "Do your work and be kind."

The Danish philanthropist is just as proud of his famous beer as he is of his famous busts and statues, paintings and water-colors. He continually reminds his co-workers — in the cause of beer and art — that the brewery that makes the profits that buy the treasures for the galleries must be conducted "irrespective of immediate gain, to

"TWO HUMAN BEINGS." BY STEPHEN SINDING

Norwegian

CARL JACOBSEN

develop its products to the greatest possible extreme of perfection, so that they may always be considered models, and insure, by their example, the manufacture of beer in Denmark being kept up to a high and honorable standard."

The altruistic attitude of men like Jacobsen is but a more vivid manifestation of the spirit of fairness that seems to pervade the social organization of the

THE NY-CARLSBERG BREWERY

"LET US LABOR FOR THE FATHERLAND"

Danish kingdom. Perhaps my optimistic view of the conditions that prevail in Copenhagen might be modified did I proceed from mere impressions to investigations of the relations between the upper and lower orders. But I hope not, for my impressions have painted for me in memory a picture of one of the happiest and most contented populations in the world.

The rich man of Copenhagen who watches the sunset from the seaside terrace of some lovely villa is not so rich that the golden splendor of the skies is lost upon him; the poor man who sits at evening beneath his humble vine and fig-tree is not so dulled by poverty that he cannot enjoy the gifts that Nature gives to every man if he will but accept them—

GUARDING THE BREWER'S GATE

sunshine and flowers, wifely glances, children's laughter, love of home, and love of Fatherland. A summer country-seat is within the reach of almost every citizen of Copenhagen. In an American city the land not built upon is represented by rubbish-strewn "vacant lots," fitting scenes

HUMBLE HOMES

for hold-ups and other deeds of darkness. In Copenhagen nearly all the vacant land in and near the completed districts is subdivided and leased for rentals, merely nominal, to laborers, mechanics, and factory hands — in short, to any wage-earners who desire to take up gardening in their leisure hours. Shanties have been evolved from stray bits of board

THE ARMY IS THERE

A POOR MAN'S VILLA

and lath and fragments of window glass. Many of these
shanties have developed into veritable villas. I show you only
two of them, but believe me when I say that we saw hundreds
of similar estates in the vast poor man's suburb that stretches

A "COUNTRY ESTATE" IN THE CITY

around Copenhagen like a broad zone of promise for the future of the city. No man knows better than the man who loves to dig in a garden the joy of labor; no man has a keener, clearer conception of the pitiful abjectness of the idleness that leads to crime. The man who loves to dig in a garden is, ten to one, a

IN AN URBAN PORT

good man; and the boy who learns to find his recreation in watching and assisting the miracles of nature in a garden is a boy saved from the city's snares and from the artificial pleasures that lead him along those slippery sidewalks of extravagance that run so perilously near the gutter. A belt of gardens cultivated by the poor is like a wall of goodness girding a metropolis. Would that the Danish emigrants who come by thousands "Direkte til Amerika" by the "Skandinavien Linie" would introduce the custom of raising peas and potatoes in our vacant lots. People laughed at Mayor Pingree, who tried to give this

A HALT FOR BEER

idea to Detroit; but the idea is a good one, good in every sense of the word; peas and potatoes are a more profitable crop than robberies and murders.

We are not surprised to learn that in Copenhagen, with a population of nearly five hundred thousand, the paupers number less than three per cent. The Danes are naturally both agricultural and maritime. We know that sixty per cent of them are farmers, and we infer from the activity that reigns along the quays in the various harbors of this splendid seaport that not a few of the remainder go often to the sea in ships. The commerce of Copenhagen surpasses in volume that of all the other Danish ports combined.

READABLE DANISH

Ships enter the canals and slips and inner harbors as if they were at home amid the houses and the public buildings of the capital. Their masts are as much local landmarks as are the towers of the quaint old town. Two of those towers are especially noteworthy. One, that of the Börs or Exchange, consists of four huge dragons, with their tails intertwined and lifted like a twisted taper toward the sky. The other, that of the Church of Our Redeemer, is circled several times by a long spiral stairway, bright with brass, which winds its three hundred and ninety-seven steps up the sharp cone to a vanishing point nearly three hundred feet above the ground. The labor of ascent is well repaid by the panorama that may be enjoyed from that extremely dizzy pinnacle. We look down on the oldest parts of Copen-

THE STAIRWAY OF THE CHURCH OF OUR REDEEMER

THE DRAGON TOWER OF THE BOURSE

hagen, attractive because the houses all have gabled roofs. A flat-roofed city, unless it be immaculately white, with house-top terraces like those of Fez or of Algiers, is always hideous. Witness a bird's-eye view of Chicago or St. Louis,

A COPENHAGEN CANAL.

a wilderness of tin-paved or gravel-covered areas adorned with water-tanks and tangled telegraph wires, bestrewn with rubbish from the garrets, and besmeared by smoke from lawless chimneys.

The biggest thing in Copenhagen was formerly the old Royal Palace of Christiansborg, its square, roofless mass looming above

COPENHAGEN GABLES

the lesser buildings like a huge hill of masonry. A more cheerless royal residence it would be hard to picture. Even when we restore it in imagination, it can seem naught but a vast, cold, and gloomy pile, a monument to the bad taste, the lack of judgment, and the pride of a weak king ruled by a silly queen, who lived about two hundred years ago. We may well doubt if even the great conflagration in 1884 succeeded in half warming the cold, cheerless corridors and halls and colonnades which, even in their roofless desolation, seem to repell sunshine and warmth. Far more inviting is the palace in which the royal family has made its home since

THE CHRISTIANSBORG PALACE

AFTER THE FIRE OF 1884

the great fire. At the four angles of a spacious square, adorned by a bronze statue of King Frederik V, rise the four pavilions of Amalienborg, each one a replica of every other, each a complete palace. Three of them are occupied, respectively, by the Minister of the Exterior, the Crown Prince, and the King; a fourth is used for coronations and state ceremonies.

The crowning feature of this royal residential quarter is the marble church, called the Frederiks-Kirke, designed by a French

THE AMALIENBORG PALACE

architect in the eighteenth century. The superb dome is sheathed in gilded copper, and though it appears to be of no great height when viewed from the octagonal *plads* in which we stand, it is still high enough to loom grandly in nearly every panorama of the city that we enjoy later from various church spires or from the tops of other Copenhagen towers.

The equestrian statue of Frederik V in this square recalls the curious fact that while Denmark found his reign an unhappy period in her history, with much poverty and a decreasing population, Norway, then subject to the Danish crown, prospered exceed-

ingly, increased in wealth and population, and surpassed Denmark in the
volume of her trade. Denmark's
comparatively unhappy condition
was, however, largely the result
of the absurdly rigid Puritanical
laws enacted during the preceding reign of the narrow-
minded Christian VI, who
tried to make his people good
by royal command, forcing
them into the churches, pro-
hibiting all the pleasures and all
the entertaining things in life.
In spite of this, surely not

FREDERIK V

because of it, the
Danes are one of the
best-behaved nations
in the world. My
impression is that
Scandinavian folk in
general, and Danish
folk in particular, are
more innately good
and honest than peo-
ple of other races!
The traveler naturally
studies faces in the
streets of foreign cities.

THE FREDERIK CHURCH

In Latin countries and in our own land, where men of every race are found, how seldom do we observe a face that leads us to exclaim, "There is a man whom I would trust implicitly!" In Scandinavia the typical face is the good, trustworthy face with a clear honest eye. Glance at the

COPENHAGEN ARCHITECTURE

passing throng in one of our great cities and tell me what is written in the majority of visages that pass. Is it frankness, open-heartedness, trustworthiness? It is far too often a look of cunning, of desire, of suspicion, of concealment, the hawk-like glance of the bird of prey, the "business look" of the man who believes in the doctrine to "do others or they will do you," or else it is the cynic's stare or the dull expression of discouragement. It may be that, misled by mere appearances, we wrong many a warm, honest heart, hid by the mask of worry and distress; nevertheless, one of the pleasures of a sojourn in Scandinavia is to meet everywhere, almost without exception, the square, clean glance of honest eyes, through which, so it appears,

good souls are looking out upon the world. Even if this be but
the traveler's fancy it is none the less refreshing to the spirit, and
none the less unusual in other countries. Go stand to-morrow
at a busy corner for ten minutes; study five hundred faces, and
count the faces that belong to people whom you decide that
you would like to know. If I were going to adopt a child without
an opportunity of looking up its pedigree, I should feel perfectly safe in picking out a Scandinavian baby. The chances
are that it would grow up good. The Danish children, while
not generally pretty, are wholesome and well-bred and polite.
Boys doff their caps and little girls will halt and curtsey to
the traveler, and even full-grown men are not ashamed to bare
the head and speed the passing traveler with a genial smile.

IN THE DOWNTOWN DISTRICT

THE VOR-FRUE-KIRKE

I know of nothing more eloquent of Danish character than the art of Denmark's greatest sculptor, Bertel Thorvaldsen. His almost countless works are housed in Copenhagen in the gallery that bears his name, the Thorvaldsen Museum.

THE THORVALDSEN MUSEUM

You know the story
of his life of labor. Born
in 1756, son of an Ice-
landic image-carver, a
maker of figureheads
for ships, he spends his
youth acquiring in crude,
simple tasks that mar-
velous facility with the
chisel that one day is to
make him famous. At
twenty-three he wins the

"NIGHT"

THREE OF
THOR-
VALDSEN'S
FAMOUS
WORKS

THE CHRIST

Grand Prize at the
Academy of Art; he is
sent to Rome to work
out his artistic salva-
tion. He returns in
1819 to Copenhagen as
the most famous sculp-
tor of his generation.
Then back to Italy he

THE
ANGEL

goes, weighted with wealth and honors,
there to continue his career, until in 1838

he comes again to his old home, bringing the marbles and the plaster models that represent a lifetime of tremendous artistic industry. Thorvaldsen's works number about five hundred. All the world knows his beautiful creations, his "Seasons," his "Night and Morning," his chastely passionate love scenes, and his tableaux of tenderness, among them the reliefs, called the "Ages of Love," which so delighted the Pope when he beheld them that his Holiness forgot to give the usual apostolic benediction on departing. Familiar, too, his later more ambitious efforts, supreme among which ranks his noble Christ, that serene figure of the Saviour which is the chief treasure of the great Church of Our Lady. But more famous than all these marbles, housed in museums or enshrined in churches, is the most noble Lion of Lucerne, memorial of the faithful Swiss who died to save King Louis the Sixteenth from the fury of the Paris populace.

BERTEL THORVALDSEN

1768–
1844

The traveler who makes even the most casual tour of Switzerland brings back with him among the most inspiring memories of peak and valley, glacier and Alpine pass, the souvenir of that wounded king of beasts, stretched in his cliff-side cave, in the throes of that death agony that has endured so many years. We always think of the Lion of Lucerne as lying there bathed in

THE LION OF LUCERNE, DESIGNED BY THORVALDSEN

IN WINTER QUARTERS

the summer sunshine or shrouded in the winter snows — life-like or death-like, but always dignified, impressive, and solitary in his suffering. But listen to the tale of two travelers who found themselves in

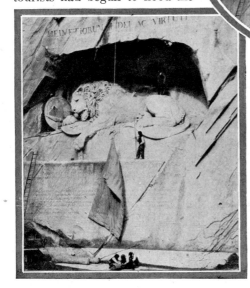

SPRING HAS COME

Switzerland in early spring, before the annual tide of tourists had begun to flood the

THE UNCOVERING OF THE LION OF LUCERNE

Alpine lakes. One morning, cold and raw, yet giving promise of the coming spring, they drew near to that famous garden in Lucerne to be alone with Thorvaldsen's Lion, that they might feel the full effect of its sad, tragic presence, so

DOMESTIC ARCHITECTURE

natural, so independent of all artificial aids. Imagine if you can their horror and astonishment, when, reaching the border of the rock-hewn pool, they are confronted by a spectacle like this: the pool is empty and the pipes that fed it are laid bare; with the aid of ladders men have invaded the cavern, which is half hid by a heavy curtain behind which lies the lion snugly wrapped, tied, tucked up, and enveloped in a dozen German feather beds! For the Lion of Lucerne is, though the world suspects it not, a hibernating animal! He spends the long cold winter sleeping under cover

A THEATER

THE ROUND TOWER

of warm comforters, his lodging screened by snow-defying curtains, and the lakelet at the cliff base drained of its contents lest the proximity of its frozen mass should bring on a case of leonine influenza!

But spring has come, and the awakening of the Lion is now in order. The thrifty Swiss are taking down the storm-door of his dwelling and removing one by one his mufflers, chest-

ON THE TOWER'S TOP

protectors, mittens, leggings, and winter flannels, and giving him his annual curry-combing to prepare him for the critical inspection of the travel-pilgrims who will soon stand in awe-stricken groups gazing across the refilled pond upon the semi-sacred and supposedly inviolable refuge of Thorvaldsen's Lion of Lucerne. I feel compunction in thus betraying the secret of this aged animal, yet you

ON THE LOUISE BRIDGE

will be rejoiced to learn that the Swiss now take these precautions annually to preserve this noble creation of Denmark's greatest sculptor from the disintegrating influences of the frost and snow of the Alpine winter.

The Lucerne Lion was the one great work of Thorvaldsen that the Danes did not try to bring to Denmark when they resolved to assemble as many as possible of the creations of their national hero-sculptor in the museum that now rises in Copenhagen as his monument and mausoleum. Nowhere else in the world is there a similarly effective monument to a beloved genius; nowhere else in the world is there so appropriate a mausoleum for a man who in his time served art to the best of his ability.

A DEVICE

Thorvaldsen sleeps beneath a simple bed of ivy in the court of the museum. In the marble halls round about the tomb are all his masterpieces — either in the original or in plaster or marble replica — from the first work that won him his opportunity, the head of Jason, to his last and unfinished work, the bust of Martin Luther.

Another famous Dane was Hans Christian Andersen, beloved by the children of a recent age when children were still children. His world-famous Fairy Tales were published first in 1836. Some boys and girls — old boys and old girls, doubtless,

THE BOAT CLUBS

ROSENBORG

now — may be amused to learn that the Danish title of their favorite childhood book was "Billedbog uden Billeder," which means a "Picture Book without Pictures." But what unforgetable pictures he made us see in that wonderful book; pictures that fed our hungry imaginations and gave substance to our early dreams. The teller of those tales died in 1875. In statued form he sits to-day in one of Copenhagen's parks — a park where children play. It is the park of the old Castle of Rosenborg. One of the towers of that fine old pile rises three

FREDERIKSBORG

hundred feet, and from its open upper floors we may look
down on Copenhagen.   King Christian IV once held royal
state at Rosenborg, but now his castle-palace is a museum
containing the very interesting chronological collection of the
Danish monarchs.   An even more interesting royal castle may
be visited in the course of a short excursion from the capital.

THE CASTLE OF FREDERIKSBORG

Artistic Denmark is epitomized in the magnificent Château
of Frederiksborg, once a royal dwelling, now a museum of Danish
arts and handicrafts.   Thorvaldsen's country is far richer than
the other Scandinavian countries in artistic monuments.   Nor is
this strange, for Denmark lies much nearer the centers of art
endeavor than Sweden or Norway, which are isolated from the
rest of Europe and occupy what is almost another continent,
joined to the mainland only at the far north, where it is soldered

IN THE COURT AT FREDERIKSBORG

by the ice of arctic uplands to the desolate wastes of Russia. The reign of Christian IV, who raised this regal Castle of Frederiksborg in the lovely forest region north of Copenhagen in the year 1620, coincided with the epoch known as the Danish Renaissance, a creative period from which dates the architectural and artistic glory of the land, and also the rise of Copenhagen to the

THE HALL OF THE KNIGHTS

BY THE SEA

rank of a great capital. The Castle of Frederiksborg is externally
one of the grandest reminders of that admirable age: internally it
tells the story of artistic evolution, for its rooms are furnished and
adorned according to the styles of the successive periods of Danish
culture, from the introduction of Christianity down to recent times.
The interest and beauty of those restored apartments reach a
culmination in the gorgeous Hall of the Knights, resplendent with

KRONBORG
CASTLE

Elsinore
Hamlet

the sheen of golden walls and ceilings, and the mirror-like radiance of polished marble pavements. And here again, amid these souvenirs of Kings whose pictured likenesses adorn the walls, the visitor of to-day, filled with the pleasure that always attends the contemplation of things that are beautiful and genuine and inter-

IN A LUTHERAN CHURCH

esting, recalls with gratitude the name of an older Jacobsen, for it was the father of the art-loving Copenhagen brewer who gave the six hundred thousand *kroner* required for the restoration of all this Middle Age magnificence. I hold no brief for brewers, but if all dispensed the profits of their breweries to as good purpose as these Danish millionaires, I could be tempted to become their advocate, enthusiastically to dissertate upon the affinity 'twixt beer and beauty, barrels and bounty, malt and magnanimity, and hops and opportunity to benefit mankind.

Only one other of the many Danish castles makes imperious call on our attention. It is Kronborg Castle, near the port of Helsingör, guarding the strait that lies between the northeastern corner of Zealand and the neighboring Swedish shore. Even to-day hundreds of ships glide in silent and continuous succession past the point where Kronborg Castle stands as sentry at the gate between the North Sea and the Baltic. But before the Kiel Canal was cut, ships to the number of twenty thousand, bound for the Russian and the Swedish ports, passed annually through this narrow channel. Denmark exacted here the Sound Dues that

yielded her so rich a profit until 1857, when the other maritime powers paid her a lump sum of about twenty million dollars, in return for which she rescinded them in perpetuity. Our country, then inconsequent commercially, was called upon for only a little more than two per cent of the sum paid — so to speak — as tribute to the land-pirates of the Skager-Rack and the coast corsairs of the Cattegat. The Castle of Kronborg has, however, another title to

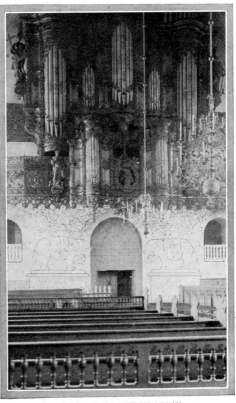

AN ARTISTIC CHURCH ORGAN

celebrity; although the names Kronborg and Helsingör are unfamiliar to the stranger, the castle is known under another name wherever Shakespeare's tongue is spoken, wherever his immortal works have made their way in any language, for it is

SHIPS PASSING ELSINORE

Hamlet's castle Elsinore! Even the fact that it was not built until long after Hamlet's day does not rob it of its fascination; we look upon the comparatively modern pile with keenest interest, for it is the Elsinore of Shakespeare's fancy. What mighty magic lies in the mere touch of genius! Elsinore would be comparatively unknown had not our glorious Shakespeare deigned to parade upon its battlemented terrace the somber figure of a melancholy Danish prince and the spirit-presence of a murdered King. The mere apparition of those same shadows of the brain of

SAILING SOUTHWARD

genius would have sufficed to give enduring famousness to
any other spot, selected at caprice by the great bard who
has given an earthly immortality to the creatures of his mighty
brain by breathing in them the breath of genius.

SEA-GULLS ATTEND US FROM PORT TO PORT

The soul of him who can give life to his creations must have
within itself some of the attributes of the Divine; and such a
soul as Shakespeare's must have experienced many earthly lives
to have learned as much as Shakespeare knew. Shakespeare is
to me the strongest argument in favor of the
theory of reincarnation. How else
could he have shown us Cæsar,
Brutus, Cassius speaking, and,
what is yet more marvelous,
thinking and feeling as men
spoke and thought and felt in
Roman days? How else could
he have made clear to us the
psychic attitude of personages
who lived and died ages ere
he was born, in countries he

A WINGED ESCORT

had never visited, unless he wrote of times in which he had once
lived and of events he half remembered — not in his mortal, perish-
able brain, but in his immortal, everlasting, and reincarnating soul?

But these, our thoughts, are like the sea-gulls that fly in our
ship's wake throughout the brief voyage we have undertaken to
another Danish port. Yet just as these birds attend us so per-

GOING TO RANDERS

sistently that we begin to look upon them as in some sense pertain-
ing to the ship herself, so, too, do certain thoughts, certain opinions
wing their way along the pathway furrowed by our minds in the
short voyage across the narrow and sometimes stormy channels of
our lives, until we come to regard them as being in some way
attached forever to the soul which they attend. And yet as
suddenly as the sea-birds that follow us across this Danish "belt"
do sometimes vanish, their places to be taken soon by other wingèd
followers, who come, we know not whence, out of the splendid
vastness of the sky, so do the worn-out thoughts and the opinions
that we have outstripped drop from the mental field of vision,

A DANISH TOWN

their places taken by sturdier, stronger thoughts, and deeper-chested, broader-winged conceptions, and these follow and attend us until, inspired by their splendid flights, we have made ourselves worthy of a still nobler following,—a flock of ideas, ideals, and opinions equipped with pinions broader still, that they may breast the gales of conscience, and soar serenely in the still, calm ether of the higher   skies of truth.

THE EXHIBITION GROUNDS AT RANDERS

We disembark after a voyage of thirteen hours from Copenhagen at the provincial port of Aarhus on the peninsula of Jutland. Provincial it may be, but not in aspect, for the main street is indicative of a metropolis. Clean, quiet, and attractive, Aarhus is the home of thirty-three thousand prosperous people who take a

SOME OF THE MACHINES ARE AMERICAN

pardonable pride in their progressive city. Were I a citizen, I should insist on showing you the monuments and public buildings, the new theater and the venerable church; but being a traveler I lead you to the railway station, whither many of the citizens are also hastening, to take a train for the neighboring town of Randers, where a famous horse-fair is held every summer. Randers is a distinctly cheerful little

DANISH SOLDIERS

JUTLAND CATTLE

town. To the sixteen thousand souls who dwell within its borders the annual horse and fat-stock show adds several thousand human and several hundred splendid equine, bovine, ovine, and porcine visitors, come from all parts of Jutland to admire and to be admired. The fair is in its third and final day,— the day of prizes, speech-making, and processions. Townsfolk and farmers throng the exhibition field, which is enlivened by hundreds of Danish flags, the sharp white cross upon a field of brightest red. As we look about us on this calmly animated scene we are struck especially by the well-to-do aspect of the people, and their grave and quiet manner.

Especially interesting to us are the superb horses, big, perfectly groomed stallions of the best Danish breed. The animals seem conscious that

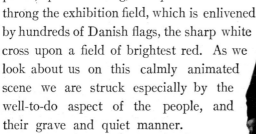

LOOKING ON

AWARDING A PRIZE

they are the most important creatures present, and pose with gravity, showing their good points to the critical onlookers, who, also with decorous gravity, gaze at these splendid specimens of equine perfection. It is indeed impressive to see what care and breeding can do for any species, and it is pitifully strange that man, who by his care has evolved these perfect equine types from the wild, shaggy creatures that once roamed the earth in savage freedom, has never thought to try the same experiment with a higher type of animal, I mean the human brute,—himself.

Apropos of physical perfection we may recall the words of George du

"HOW'S THAT FOR HIGH!"

Maurier, who, in his wonderful book, "Peter Ibbetsen,"
referring to the perfect human types represented by the Elgin marbles from the
Parthenon, exclaimed: "But the splendor
of the Elgin marbles! I understood that
at once, perhaps because there is not so
much to understand. Mere physically
beautiful people appeal to us all,
whether they be in flesh or marble. . . . By some strange intuition

A SPLENDID MANE

I knew that people
ought to be built
like that; before
I had
ever seen a single statue in that
wondrous room I had divined
them, so completely did they
realize an esthetic ideal
I had always felt. I
had often peopled an
imaginary world of my
own with a few hundreds

powerful horses!

POSING

of such beings made flesh
and blood, and pictured
them as a kind of
beneficent aristoc-
racy, seven feet
high, with minds
and manners to
match their phy-
sique, and set
above the rest of
the world for its

PRIZE-WINNERS AT RANDERS

"YES, I SPEAK ENGLISH"

good!" And in another place he utters this incisive truth: "They are such people as we should all be had it not been for the lack of a little care and self-denial on the part of a few hundreds of millions of our ancestors!" Man studies carefully the proper nourishment for the prize-winning brutes,— the horses, bulls, and pigs that he sends to exhibitions like this famous Randers Fair, but he usually feeds himself — human contestant for the prize of happiness — upon the most unfit of foods, and pours into his system all sorts of liquid poisons. Unthinking man, to take pride in rearing healthy horses seventeen hands high, and at the same time feel no shame that he and his own children fall so far short of that physical perfection that should be the right and portion of us all! No wonder that the happy horses on which we look at Randers appear to regard puny, ill-shapen man with an air of serene superiority.

The presentation of prizes and diplomas takes place late in the afternoon. Horses, bulls, cows, sheep, and hogs are led by their proud owners past the tribune, where the Burgomaster bestows

JUST ONE WORD

the merited awards, adding a few words of compliment in Danish. I want to say a word about the Danish language, and one word ought to suffice if I could find a word in English to equal, in point of sesquipedalianism, the one word that we saw upon the sign-

RURAL DENMARK

board of a public institution. It was "Industriforeningsbygningen!" But failing to find such a word in our language, let me confine myself to saying that fortunately the traveler need not know even a half word of Danish in order to enjoy a journey through the interior of Denmark, for in every group of

PRETTY AS A PICTURE

Danes he will find two or three who speak the English language with reassuring fluency. Even at Randers, far from the routes of tourist travel, at least a dozen men voluntarily came to offer their assistance to us strangers, addressing us in perfect English. Among them was one kindly farmer who had brought his boys

OUR EARLIEST AUTO . . .

to see the show, and took great pleasure in showing them that he had not forgotten English, though he had not used a word of it for fifteen years. At Randers one might well expect to hear the Anglo-Saxon tongue, for that is the language of the horsey man from David Harum to Tod Sloan. But we found even in the remoter villages that English words and phrases were familiar. The children can almost invariably understand and answer our questions, the old folks have nearly all at least a vague book-knowledge of our tongue, while

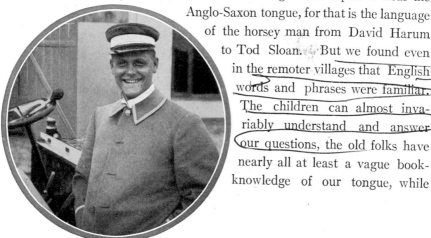

. . . AND OUR MILITARY CHAUFFEUR

IN A DANISH GARDEN

not a few of the young men and women are prosperous Danish-Americans returned from Illinois, Wisconsin, or Ohio.

Our thoroughly delightful association with the Danes of rural districts was brought about, thanks to a French automobile and a tall, handsome military chauffeur, both belonging to a colonel in the Danish army who placed them at our disposition for a tour up, down, and across the lovely isle of Zealand. Happy, indeed, the morning that saw us fairly started for the first long automobile tour that it had ever been my fortune to enjoy.

There were few motor cars in Denmark at that time; ours was in fact the only one that had the proper rakish cut. But wonderful as it was even to us, I may as well confess that it would excite only ridicule to-day, for it was a mere six horse-power *voiturette*, capable of twenty-five miles an hour on the level roads, but rather weak and puffy when it came to climbing hills, of which there were, however, very few along our way. You know the joyful feeling born of speed, and we indeed were as joyful as our cheery-faced chauffeur, whose smile, as you may see on glancing

GOOD ROADS

at his portrait, was a most
contagious smile. A
typical son of Den-
mark he; cheery
and clean and
wholesome as a
well-bred boy;
honest, capable
and courageous
as the Danish sol-
dier that he is — for
the chauffeur is a mili-
tary man in command of
the auto car furnished us

NEW TO THEM

by the colonel of his regiment. On we go, past trees and fields
and houses, tasting the sweet delights of speed, all the more sweet
because those indescribable delights are new to us. We are be-
ginners, receiving our baptism of velocity; glorying in our initiation into the Order of the Knights of Speed. I am just
preparing to put on that badge of the brotherhood, a ferocious big
pair of goggles, when suddenly a new phase of our initiation bursts

upon us, —bang!
pss-s-ss!   You
know the rest —

Off with your coats,
  Out with the tools,
Down on your knees,
  Feeling like fools.
Jack up the wheel,
  Tear off the tire,
Pull out the tube —
  Toil and perspire.
Plug up the holes,
  Gum up the gaps;
Prepare to meet
  Other mishaps.

Then to the joy
of ourselves and
the local juve-

GIVING A LADY A LIFT

niles, off we go again, happy to have the trouble over with so
early in the day.   A fine straight stretch of perfectly smooth road
extends its tempting band of white, edged with green, as far as we
can see.   Full speed ahead once more, and we settle back into

THE VILLAGERS

TROUBLE

the leathery embrace of the tonneau, and I again prepare to don
those dust-defying goggles, with the same result, bang! pss-s-ss!
Oh, the horror of that sound, the hiss of that elastic serpent
coiled around the right rear wheel, that flabby rubber viper that

KINDLY INTEREST

will not hold its
breath long enough
for us to cover half
a kilometer! But
happily the tele-
phone is every-
where in Denmark.
We call up the
only auto shop in
Copenhagen, and
with a promptitude
that would put to

shame a fire engine or an ambulance, an emergency motor comes
rushing to our rescue, bringing a new tire out from town, and
before we can adjust it a second relief expedition is signaled by
a cloud of dust, and soon our wrecking party is working under

the orders of the proprietor of the shop, who has come all the way from town merely, as he says, "to make sure that the American gentlemen have a good day." Thanks to his aid and that of his willing men, things are soon put to rights and we do have a good day, one of the best days that we can remember, unless it be the day that followed, and the day that followed that. Denmark,

VORDINGBORG

however, is too small a country for a satisfying spin. If the chauffeur is not careful he will run right off the edge! Almost before we realize that we have covered nearly ninety miles we roll into the small city of Vordingborg at the south extremity of Zealand. There from the tower of a ruined castle we look down on the peaceful port where our auto tour would have come to an end had we not learned that there was a steam ferry not far off, by means of which we could effect an auto-invasion of the neighboring isle of Möen, its roads as yet unpressed by rapid rubber tires. We are compelled to charter the ferry for a special trip. The regular fare is very low, like everything in Denmark, but of

south of Copenhagen

course a special and higher rate is made for us, and in exchange for a bank note of the required denomination the captain, who speaks perfect English, presents us with several yards of paper ribbon, composed of receipt coupons, scores of them being required to represent the enormous sum we have paid,—three dollars.

THE MÖEN LANDSCAPE

Möen is a lovely little island, an ideal out-of-the-way corner, peaceful and prosperous and pretty, its perfumed air sweet with the sweetness of the new-mown hay, never before polluted by the breath of a malodorous motor. It seems almost a sacrilege, this motor-car invasion of an Arcadian island. We feel almost ashamed

THE FIRST MOTOR FERRIED TO MÖEN

of being so barbarously up to date, so alien in attitude to the
good folk of Möen, who scarcely pay us the scant compliment
of curiosity. To them the making of their hay is a concern
more vital than the advent of a new-fangled engine in a region to
which even the railroad is a stranger. We did expect that the
police of Stege, the only town through which we passed, would
read the riot act to us, because we had been warned that even
though the men of Möen have never seen an automobile they
have already framed a code of laws to cope with the new nuisance.
But though we halted opposite the small town hall and ostenta-
tiously replenished the tanks, the warning finger of authority was
not lifted, and we sped toward the remoter and more peaceful
eastern coast, over roads narrower than those over which auto-

IDLE WINGS

PEACEFUL DENMARK

mobiles are, according to the new law, allowed to roam. Our pleasure is marred only by the constantly recurring instants of anxiety that come to us, poor unsophisticated chauffeurs that we are, every time we meet a skittish team of horses. Of course we should not let a little thing like that annoy us, but the man who possesses the unhappy faculty of putting himself in the other fellow's place will never break speed records on a public highway. But the other fellow does not seem to think that we are foolish to stop, when we see his distress and hear the anxious little shrieks from his frightened women folk. On the

ONE OF MANY COUNTRY CHURCHES

contrary, he invariably thanks us with a grateful "*taka taka,*" and
lifts his hat as soon as he can spare a hand to do so.   The family
parties encountered every mile or two are on their way to one of
the many churches which form such pleasing features in the
landscape.   As Christians we approved the churchward tendency
of the rural population, but as chauffeurs we found it far from

GABLES AND TOWERS OF STAIRWAY DESIGN

gratifying; and yet it was a pleasure to see so many happy, well-
dressed folk abroad, always in family groups,—old folk and
middle-aged folk and children of all ages togged out in Sunday-go-
to-meeting clothes with sober Sunday smiles upon their honest
faces.   We halted at one farm house to beg a pail of water for
the over-heated thirsty monster that bore us now so unfalteringly
southward.   Kindly and courteous, the boys fetch brimming
pails, and all watch the water disappear down the brass gullet of
the mysterious metal brute.   Their questions prove that they
have read about this new mode of locomotion; their curiosity is
intelligent, for rural Denmark reads the papers, and the country

MAKING HAY

boy is as well informed as his city cousin. It is said that the Danes are first cousins to the English, but I doubt if any Danish school boy would be guilty of the errors of sense and nonsense revealed by a competition recently instituted in London by an English periodical publication. It seems that English teachers are so used to absurd answers from stupid or thoughtless boys that they have a name for these startlingly comic replies to examination questions; they call them "How- lers," and perusing the following list of "Howlers" you will un- derstand the why and

DANISH DAIRY-MAIDS

wherefore of the term. Behold the workings of the boyish British brain:

Women's suffrage is the state of suffering to which they were born.

Lord Raleigh was the first man to see the Invisible Armada.

REAL DANES

Shakespeare founded "As You Like It" on a book previously written by Sir Oliver Lodge.

Tennyson wrote "In Memorandum."

George Eliot left a wife and children to mourn his genii.

WHERE BREAD WEARS THE CROWN

THE FARMER . . .

King Edward IV had no claim by geological right to the English throne.

Henry I died of eating palfreys.

Louis XVI was gelatined during the French Revolution.

The Rhine is boarded by wooden mountains.

An angle is a triangle with only two sides.

Parallel lines are

. . . AND HIS FAMILY

the same distance all the way, and do not meet unless you bend them.

A vacuum is a large empty space where the Pope lives.

Martin Harvey invented the circulation of the blood.

Geometry teaches us how to bisex angles.

HOME, SWEET HOME

The whale is an amphibious animal because it lives on land and dies in the water.

A parallelogram is a figure made of four parallel straight lines.

Horse-power is the distance one horse can carry a pound of water in an hour.

The press to-day is the mouth-organ of the people.

SOME OF THE NEIGHBORS

Algebraical symbols are used when you don't know what you are talking about.

A deacon is the lowest kind of Christian.

The isles of Greece were always quarreling as to which was the birthplace of Homer: Chaos has the most right to claim him.

A FARM HOUSE

But meantime we have been visiting a peasant cottage. There was nothing crude or primitive about the rural home we entered, at the invitation of the prosperous farmer to whom the adjacent fields belonged. The interior indicated comfort, thrift, simplicity of life, and peace of mind. It may be taken as a type of the home of the small farmer in the south of Denmark.

Denmark is a land of little farms — little as compared with farms as measured in America. It is even interdicted by law to join together a number of small farms to form a large estate. The large landowner, on the other hand, is encouraged to subdivide his holdings among many tenants, and every tenant has entire control of the land he occupies so long as the rental is paid.

Eighty per cent of the area of Denmark is productive. The rest is not without its value, for peat bogs cover most of it, and, as in Ireland, peat is the common fuel in many of the villages.

A BUTTER FARM

There is a little forest land, but the meadow and the pasture are conspicuously characteristic of the Danish landscape.

Cattle are of course the farmer's first concern. Denmark is one vast park-like pasture, a rolling grazing ground with a range of cows on every ridge. Denmark sends fifty million dollars' worth of butter to Great Britain every year. How much goes forth to other countries I do not know, but I do know that Danish butter, put up in tins, is famous the wide world over. I have spread Danish butter on my bread in many far-off countries. We carried it by caravan into Morocco, and even after many days under the African sun we found it fresh and sweet when we opened the cans in Fez, the Moors' metropolis. We laid it thick upon our Grecian bread in Thessaly, while living up in a Meteora monastery in air. Long ago in Japan, in the remote interior villages, my never-to-be-forgotten "boy," Tsuni Horiuchi, used Danish butter in the making of his famous omelettes. But when we brought Danish butter with us into Siberia on the occasion of

THE INN AT LISELUND

our first and seemingly interminable journey from the Urals to the Pacific, we found that we were bringing it to its old home — for much of the butter tinned in Denmark and labeled "Best Danish" comes originally from the western regions of Siberia. It is a pretty crude and not too clean a product as it comes from the Siberian mujik's farm; but in Denmark it is scientifically clarified and purified before going into the neat tin boxes in which it journeys to the ends of the earth, to delight the civilized palate in many a far-away uncivilized or barbarous land.

It is always interesting to approach the source of any famous

canned butter

product. Accordingly we draw near with alacrity to a maiden who is milking a fine Danish cow, observing that the maiden is not unattractive. Nor is she in the least flattered by our attention. She does not interrupt her work; mechanically, almost automatically, she continues to draw from the patient animal with her skilful fingers that juice of the green earth, that generous essence of these grass-covered acres that is to be transformed into Danish butter. Grain-raising also flourishes, and Danish bread is worthy of the Danish butter spread upon it, or of the good milk into which it may be dipped. Corn may be king us, but it is wears the Denmark. every shop there sort of with bread that crown in In front of baker's hangs a twisted loaf, a giant pretzel with a gilded diadem upon what may be termed its brow — if pretzels may be said to have a brow. Wholesome as bread and butter is this land through which our machine rushes. Unmolested we arrive at Liselund, our destination. Our stay, however, must

YOUNG DENMARK

be brief, for we must set out for the return journey early the next morning. Yet it were a pity not to see the famous sights of Möen, called the Lille and the Store Klint. Klint means cliff. A range of pure white promontories jutting seaward from the forest-covered coast of Möen is the only striking scenic feature of all Denmark. But those cliffs are several miles away from Lise-lund, and it is already late, past six o'clock. This matters little in a latitude where the summer sun sets after nine and the twilight lasts till morning; so off we trudge on foot along the darkening road to seek the only startling scenery in Denmark. We tramp and tramp, and still the cliffs are far away. Then my companion, tired out, turns back, while I go on. For two weary hours I stumbled on, as I supposed, toward those white

cliffs which I ex-pected every minute would lift their gleaming masses beyond the next turn of the vague path I was following. Eight miles or so of this and still no sign of cliff or sea, or of the path, for even it had disap-peared entirely. The horrid sense of being lost grips me, and when I shout aloud the sound of my own voice is more awful than the silence

NEAR THE KLINT

THE CLIFFS OF MÖEN

and the solitude. Comfort, however, comes in the thought that Denmark is a very little country, and Möen a very little island and that its tiny forest cannot long enshroud a bewildered wanderer who energetically seeks an issue from its mazes.

So back the wanderer turns, and after several hours of suspense finds himself safe and sound at Liselund. Therefore must I confess that our trip to Liselund to see the cliffs of Möen was barren of result. The "only scenery in Denmark" was not seen at all by your chagrined and disappointed deputy. The pictures of it must be credited to other cameras

THE CREST OF THE KLINT

only scenery in Denmark

than his. But after all our tour has not been profitless, for we have seen a land rich in content and kindliness and peace. Because we failed to see and to enjoy Denmark's most famous scenic sight proves not the failure of the journey; and as it is with our journeys, so it is with our lives. Because we fail to touch the summits of existence, to reach high places in the world, proves not the failure of life. The enduring joys of the journey that leads us over the smooth and peaceful lowlands of content are really more to be desired than the ephemeral satisfactions, born of excursions to the cruel cliffs of pride, or to the jagged summits of extravagance. May our life-journey lead us out from the dark woods, through which we have groped so blindly toward the things that cannot satisfy, out into the glorious open fields of labor and rewarded effort, where we may reap — not all at once — but *every day a little* of the harvest of our happiness.

Index to This Volume

NOTE.—In the Scandinavian languages the vowels *a, e, i* are pronounced *ah, ay, ee,* as in French and German; *o* long is pronounced like *o* in *pole,* and when short somewhat like *o* in *dot; ai, ei, oi* are diphthongs; *u* long is like *u* in *mute,* rarely like the *o* in *move,* when short like *u* in *urn; y* long is like the German *ü,* when short it is the same as *ϕ,* which corresponds to the German *ö* or the French *eu.* The Swedish *å̄ (aa* in Norwegian and Danish) has the sound of *a* in *ball.*

The consonants, with a few exceptions, are like the English. The principal exceptions follow: *f* at the end of a word is pronounced like *v; g,* before *i* and *e* and also at the end of a syllable frequently has the consonant sound of *y; j* always has the sound of the consonant *y, k,* followed by *e, i, j, y, æ* or *ϕ,* is pronounced (in Norway) like the English *ch; d* and *g* are usually silent at the end of a word or syllable.

Aarhus, *awr'hoos,* Denmark, 310.

Åbo, *ah'bo,* (in Swedish, *aw'bo*), once capital of Finland, 232.

Alcohol, Norway's war against, 31-35.

Alexander I, tsar of Russia, 237-238.

Alexander II, tsar of Russia, 238.

Andersen, Hans Christian, 299-300.

Archer, Colin, designer of the "Fram," 94.

Architecture:
Danish, 282-283.
Norwegian, 17, 18-21.
Swedish, 151-152, 181-182, 197.

Army:
Finnish, 241, 243.
Swedish, 150, 174.

Auks, near polar regions, 97-98.

Automobile, trip through Zealand, 317-326.

Baltespannare, Molin's statue of belt-dwellers, 141-143.

"Baron von Platen," Swedish canal steamer, 131.

Bars, Norwegian regulations for, 32-35.

Bathing, prejudice against, Norway, 68-69.

Beauty, market value of, 182.

Beds, Norwegian, 67.

Bellman, Karl, national poet of Sweden, 159.

Belt Duel, Molin's statue of, 141-143.

Bergen, *bur'gen,* Norway:
"Club Life," 35.
Contrasts of old and new, 30-31.
Fires, 35-36.
History, 28-30.
Museums, 36.
Population, 29.
Rainfall, 35.

Bernadotte, *ber'nah dot,* Marshall, founder of house of Ponte Corvo, 156.

Birger Jarl, *yarl,* Swedish chieftain, 151.

Birgitta, *bir git'tah,* Swedish saint, 133-134.

Björnson, *byurn'sun,* Björnstjerne, most popular personage in Norway, 9.

Blood Bath, the, 167.

Blue Laws, in Gotland, 220-221.

Boats, Posting, on the fjords, 43.

Bokrikoff, governor of Finland, 242.

Bränvinsbord, Swedish gastronomic institution, 131-132.

Bremer, *braym'er,* Frederika, 160.

Bridget, Saint, Swedish, 133-134.

Bull, Ole, story of, 36-37.

Butter, Danish, 331-333.

Cafés, Stockholm, 147-149.

Canals, Swedish. See *Göta.*

Cattle, raising, in Denmark, 331-333.

Charles the Twelfth, king of Sweden, 170-173.

Chauffeur, Danish, 317-318.

Children, Norwegian, 16-17.

Christian II, 167.

Christian VI, king of Denmark, 287.

Christian IX, king of Denmark, 262-263.

Christiania, to Hardanger Fjord, overland trip, 21-28.

Churches:
Denmark, 282, 286, 325.
Norway, 18, 80-81.
Sweden, 133-134, 173, 205-206, 214, 221.

Cleanliness, Norway a land of, 69.

"Club Life," absence of, Norway, 35.

Coast Line, Norway's, 41.

Cod:
Fishing from the steamer, 99-100.
Great Cod Catch, 90-91.

Colorado River, Grand Cañon of the, 6.

Copenhagen, *koh pen hay'gen,* Denmark:
Attractiveness, 266-267.
Castles and palaces, 284-286, 300-301.
Commerce, 281-282.
Elevators, up-to-date, 267-268.
Gardening, 277-281.
Museums, 270-273.
Population, 281, 301.
Tivoli Garden 268-269.

Cossacks, in Finland, 243.

Council of State, Swedish cabinet, 144.

"Courts of Mutual Agreement," Norway, 48-49.

Cronstadt, Russian fortress, 233-234.

Dalarne, *dah lahr'neh,* or **Dalecarlia,** *dah le kar'lee ah,* heart of the Swedish fatherland, 196-200.

Day, a meaningless term in northern Norway, 96.

Democracy, spirit of Sweden, 157-159.

Denmark (in Danish, *Danmark*):
Aarhus, 310.
Area and population, 263-264.
Architecture, 282-283.
Artistic development, 301-304.
Character of the people, 287-289.
Colonies, 165-266.
Copenhagen, the capital. See that title.
Farms, 330-333.
Government, 263.
History, 260-263, 286-287.
Language, 315.
Randers, horse-fair, 310-315.
Scenery, 334-335.
Stege, 323.
Zealand, trip through, 317-336.

Diets, national:
Denmark, 263.
Finland, 238, 241.
Sweden, 144.

Djupvand, *dyoop'vahnd,* Norwegian lake, 56-57.
Post-station on shore, 57.

Dress:
Norwegian, 18.
Swedish, 183-185, 197-200.

Drottningholm, *drot'ning hohlm,* Queen's Island, summer palace of king of Sweden, 135.

Dynasty, ruling, established in Norway, 7.

Education, in Sweden, 173, 195.

Eidfjordvand, *ide fyord vahnd,* Norway's grandest glacial lake, 23.

Elevators, in Copenhagen's city hall, 267-268.

Emigration, from Finland, 242.

English, spoken in Denmark, 315-317.

Ericson, Leif, the Viking, 94.

Ericsson, John, Swedish engineer, 131, 251.

Farming, in Norway, 76-78.

"Fast Skyds Station," Norwegian post service, 57.

Fat Katerina, *kah ter ee'nah,* famous tower in Viborg, 254.

Feudal System, lack of foothold in Norway, 13-14.

Finland, the land of the Finns:
Abo, 232.
Army, 241, 243.
Ceded to Russia, 118.
Civilized corner of tsar's domain, 256.
Cronstadt, fortress, 233-234.
Emigration, 242.
Geology, 230-231.
Government, 235-236, 243.
Helsingfors, 234-235.
History, 236-243.
Lake region, 250-251.
Language, 228-229.
Literature, 244-249.
Race, 225-228.

Finsen, Niels, winner of Nobel prize, 162.

Fishing, trout and salmon, Norway, 79-80.

Fjeldvei, mountain drive at Bergen, 28.

Fjords, *fyords:*
Boat service, 43.
Cables across, 43.
Geiranger, 60.
Geology, 44-47.
Naero Fjord, 43.
Nord Fjord, 53.
Norwegian, 40-47.
Sogne Fjord, 40.

"For Norge Kjaempers Föderland," national anthem of Norway, 54.

"Fram," *frahm,* Nansen's Arctic ship, 94.

Frederik V, king of Denmark, 286-287.

Frederick VIII, king of Denmark, 8, 261.

Frederiksborg, Château, Danish museum, 301-304.

Fuglo, *foo'glo,* island in Northern Norway, 107-109.

Gardens, in Copenhagen, 277-281.

Geiranger, *gy'rane yer,* fjord, Norway, 60, 63-64.

George I, king of Greece, 8.

George V, king of England, 8

Glaciers, Norway, 24-25.

Göta, *gû'tah,* (the *u* as in *urn*), river and canal system, Sweden.
Baron von Platen, 130.
Canal system, 126-129.
Polhem's lock, 122.

River, 122.
Visitor's book, of stone, 125.
Water power, 122, 125.
Gothenburg, *got'en berg,* (in Swedish, Göteborg, *yew tee bor'y'*):
Importance, 119.
Liquor traffic, 120-122.
Gothenburg System:
Introduced into Norway, 32.
Sweden, 120-122.
Gotland, *gote'lahnd,* Swedish province:
Blue Laws, 220-221.
Churches, 212-214, 220-221.
Former wealth, 206, 218.
History and legend, 208-212, 214-218.
Population, 208.
Spirits' plague, 218-220.
Superstitions, 214-218.
Trip to, 200-203.
Visby and the Hanseatic League, 203-214.
Great Cod Catch, in the Lofoten Fjords, 90-91.
Grieg, *greeg,* Edvard, composer, 9-10.
Grotlid Road, journey over the, 56-63.
Gudbrandsdal, *good'brahnds dahl,* valley, Norway, 75.
Gudvangen, *good vahngen,* a Norwegian port, 50.
Gulls, near polar regions, 97-98.
Gustaf V, *goos'tahv,* king of Sweden, 156.
Gustaf-Adolf, crown prince of Sweden, 157.
Gustavus Adolphus:
Career, 168-169.
Founded Gothenburg, 119.
Gustavus Vasa, *vah'sah,* king of Sweden, 164-168.
Guti, *goo'ti,* king of Jutland, 211.
Haakon VII, *haw'kone,* king of Norway, 7-8.
Hamlet, castle of, Elsinore, 306-307.
Hammerfest, *hahm'er fest,* the midnight sun metropolis, 96-97.
Hangö, *hahng'geh,* Finnish fort, 232-233.
Hanse, meaning of the word, 30.
Hanseatic League, 29-30, 204-207.
Hawaii, *hah wy'ee,* resemblance of Finnish names to, 230.
Hay, drying on fences, Norway, 77.
Hedin, *hay'deen,* Sven, Swedish explorer, 161.
Helgeandsholm, *hel yay ahnds hohlm,* island in Stockholm, 143-144.

Hell, a Norwegian town:
Englishwoman's joke, 84-85.
Excursion to, 82-84.
Meaning of the name, 84.
Helsingfors, Finland, 234-235.
Hesjer, *hays'yare,* hay fences, Norway, 77.
Honesty and Courtesy, of Scandinavians, 37-39, 287-289.
Horses:
Norwegian, 14, 57-58.
Randers fair, 310-315.
Hotels:
Norway, 37-38, 66-68, 70.
Sweden, 139.
"Howlers," comic replies to examination questions, 326-330.
Hullet of Torghattan, 86-89.
Ibsen, Henrik, 9.
Ice, miracle worker in Norway, 6-7.
Imatra, falls of, Finland, 250.
Jacobsen, *yah'kob sen,* Carl, Copenhagen philanthropist, 270-276.
Japanese, related to the Finns, 226.
Jews, in Norway, 48.
Jungfrutorn, *yoong'froo torn,* the Maiden's Tower, Visby, 209-210.
"Kalevala," *kah le vah'lah,* Finnish epic, 244-248.
Key, *kye,* Ellen, Swedish author, 160.
Kiel, *keel,* German port, 264.
Klinte, cliffs of Gotland, 221-222.
Klokstapel, steeple at Skansen, Sweden, 186-189.
Korsör, *kor'sir,* Danish port, 265.
Kovalevsky, *ko vahl ef'ski,* Sonia, 160.
Kronborg Castle, *krone'borg,* Denmark, 305-307.
Ladoga, *lah'do gah,* Russian lake, 250.
Lagerlöf, *lah'ger lef,* Selma, 160, 162.
Lapps, 94-95.
"Last-born Daughter of the Sea," Finland, 230-231.
Leif Ericson, the Viking, 94.
Lind, Jenny, 160.
Linnæus, *lin nee'us,* Swedish naturalist, 161, 177.
Lion of Lucerne, 292-298.
Liquor Traffic, controlled by Gothenburg system, 120-122.
Liselund, *lee'se loond,* Denmark, 333, 335.
Literature:
Finnish, 244-249.
Norwegian, 9.
Swedish, 159-160.
Loen Vand, *lo'en vahnd,* grandest lake in Norway, 53-54.

Lofoten Islands, *loh fo'ten*, Norway, 90-91.

Lorsday, Lord's Day, in the suburbs of Stockholm, 179-180.

Lucerne, *loo sern'*, lion of, 292-298.

Lützen, battle of, 169.

Lyngen Fjord, most beautiful of Nordland gulfs, 105-107.

Maabödal, *maw bö dahl*, Norwegian valley, 23.

Magerö, *mah'ge rö*, island of the North Cape, 99.

Magyars, *mod'yorz*, related to Finns, 226.

Mälaren, *may'lahr en*, Lake, Sweden, 135, 147.

Merok, *may'rok*, Norway, 61-63.

Midnight Sun, The, 102-105, 107-111.

Mö'en, isle and cliffs of Denmark, 321-326, 334-336.

Molin, Swedish sculptor, 141.

Museums:
Copenhagen, 270-273, 301.
National museum, Franklin Smith's plans, 190-192.
Skansen, Sweden, 185-190.
Stockholm, 141.

Music:
Norway:
Grieg, Edward, 9-10.
Sinding, Christian, 10.
Sweden:
Jenny Lind and Christine Nilsson, 160.

Naerodal, Norwegian fjord, 44, 50-52.

Naes, entrance to the Romsdal, 70.

Nansen, Fridtjof, Arctic explorer, 94.

Nature:
Extravagance in Norway, 5-6.
Cruelty, 77-78.

Navy, Swedish, 174.

"Neptune," Norwegian steamer, 86.

Nicholas II, tsar of Russia, attitude toward Finland, 241-243.

Night, a meaningless term in northern Norway, 96.

Nights, glorious, in Finland, 251.

Nilsson, Christine, 160.

Nobel, Alfred, and the Nobel prizes, 161-163.

Nobility:
Norway, abolition in, 13.
Sweden, 157.

Nordenskjold, *nor'den shöl*, Nils Adolf, Swedish explorer, 161.

Nord Fjord, Norway, 53.

Norrbro, focal point of Stockholm life, 149-150.

North Cape, 98-99, 101-102.

Northern Museum, Stockholm 193-194.

Norway (in Norwegian, *Norge*):
Architecture, 17-21.
Bergen. See that title.
Character of people, 13-17, 37-39, 64-65, 78-79.
Children, 16-17.
Christiania, 21.
Coast line, 41.
Courts of mutual agreement, 48-49.
Democracy, 8.
Dress, 18.
Emigration, 12.
Farming, 76-78.
Fishing, 79-80.
Fjords, 40-47, 53, 60, 63-64.
Geology, 6-7.
Hammerfest, 96-97.
History, 7-8, 13-14, 29-30, 91-94.
Hotels, 66-68, 70.
Lakes. See that title.
Manners and customs, 16-18, 64, 67.
Midnight sun, 102-105, 107-111.
National anthem, 54.
North Cape, 98-99, 101-102.
Population, 12-13.
Railways, 26-28.
Religion, 47-48.
Scenery unparalleled, 10-11, 63-64, 89-90.
Spirits' Plague, 31-35.
Travel, conditions of, 41-43.
Trondhjem, 80-81.
Vehicles, 14-16, 52.
Women, 13, 54-56.

Odde, *ohd'deh*, Norwegian seaport town, 22.

Olaf, *oh'lahf*, Norwegian saint, 217-218.

Oscar II, king of Sweden, 135, 157.

Painting, Otto Sinding, 10.

Palaces:
Copenhagen, 284-286.
Stockholm, 152-155.

Paris of the North, Stockholm, 137-139.

Paupers, in Copenhagen, 281.

Peasantry, condition in Sweden, 157-158.

Platen, Baron von, Swedish promoter, 130.

Police, Stockholm, 174.

Ponies, Norwegian, 58.

Postage Stamps, black, issued by Finland, 241-242.

Post-road, "the Winter Way," 232.

Post stations, Norway, 57.

Railways:
Norway, 26-28.
Sweden, 144.
Rainfall, Bergen, 35.
Randers, *rahn'ders*, scene of a famous horse-fair, 310-315.
Rauma, river, Norway, 75.
Reindeer, reared by the Lapps, 95.
Religion:
Norway, part in the life of the people, 47-48.
Sweden, 173.
Rembedals-vand, Norwegian lake, 24-26.
Renaissance, Danish, 302-303.
Riddarholm Church, mausoleum of the Swedish kings, 173.
Seven Sisters, most famous of the Geiranger waterfalls, 64.
Shakespeare, 306-308.
Siljan, *sil'yahn*, Lake, in the heart of Sweden, 199-200.
Simodal, Norway, 23-26.
Sinding, the three brothers, 10.
Skansen, museum of Swedish life, 185-190.
Skärgård, *skair'gawrd*, Swedish coast, 201-202.
Skjoergaard, Norwegian islands, 39.
Smith, Franklin, plan for a series of national museums, 190-192.
Smörgåsbord, a Swedish gastronomic institution, 131-132.
Södra Blasieholmshamnen, Stockholm, 140-141.
Sogne Fjord, *sog'ne fyord*, longest in Norway, 40.
Soldiers, Swedish, 150, 174.
"Spirits' Plague," Norway's struggle against, 31-35.
Gotland, 218-220.
Staden, *stah'den*, island in Stockholm, 143.
Stalheims-Klev, *stahl himes kleff*, view of the Naerodal, 50-52.
"Starboard," origin of the term, 91.
Stav Churches, Norway, 18.
Steamers:
Norwegian:
Fjords, service on, 43.
Rates of fare, 47.
Swedish, 233.
Stege, *stay'geh*, town in Denmark, 323.
Stockholm, Sweden:
Compared with Venice, 135-136.
Cafés, 147-149.
Elegance and refinement, 137-139.
Hotels, 139.
Location, 135-136, 200.
National Museum, 141.
Norrbro, 149-150.
Opera House, 147.
Palace, 143, 151, 155.
Police, 174.
Population, 136.
Riksdag building, 143-144.
Soldiers, 150.
Suburbs, 177-182.
Telephone system, 174-176.
Strömparterre, Stockholm, 147-148.
Suburbs, Stockholm, 177-181.
Suffrage:
Denmark, 263.
Finland, 235-236.
Sweden, 118, 144.
Sunsets, Finland, 251.
Suomi, *soo oh'mee*, native name of Finns, 243.
Sweden (in Swedish, Sverige, *svair'-ih gay*):
America, Swedes in, 115-116.
Army, 150, 174.
Blue Laws, 220-221.
Canals, 122-131.
Character of the people, 117, 222-224.
Dalarne, heart of the fatherland, 196-200.
Democracy, 157-159.
Dress, 183-185, 197-200.
Education, 173, 195.
Gothenburg, 119-122.
Gotland. See that title.
Government, 144.
History, 117-119, 151, 156-157, 164-173, 211.
Literature, 9.
Manners and customs, 131-132, 202.
Museums. See that title.
Navy, 174.
Nobel Prizes, 161-163.
Peasantry, 157-158.
Population, 117.
Railways, 144.
Religion, 173.
Royal family, 156-157.
Skansen, national museum, 185-190.
Stockholm. See that title.
Visby. See that title.
Swedenborg, 160-161.
Tegnér, *teg nair'*, Esaias, Swedish poet, 159.
Telemarken District, Norway:
Architecture, 17.
Wedding customs, 17-18.

Telephone, Stockholm system, 174-176.

Tessin, Nicodemus, father and son, builders of Drottningholm, 135.

Theater, Royal Opera House, Stockholm, 147.

Thorwaldsen, *tor'vahld zen*, Bertel, Danish sculptor, 290-292, 298-299.

Tjällver, legend about, 210-211.

Torghattan, the island with a hole in it, 86-89.

Towers, two famous, Copenhagen, 282.

Troldtinder, needles of the Trolls, Romsdal, 71.

Trolls, the Norwegian, 71-72.

Trondhjem, *trond'yem*, Norway:
Cathedral, 80-81.
Shocking signs, 81.
Nucleus of Norway, 80.

Trout, fishing in Norway, 79-80.

Tsar of Russia, overlord of Finland, 236-243.

Ugrian, *oo'gri an*, ethnological group, 226-228.

United States, similarity to Sweden, 194-195.

Upsala, *oop sah'lah*, University, Sweden, 173.

Vadstena, *vahd stay'nah*, Swedish town, 133-134.

Valdemar, *vahl'de mahr*, king of Denmark, 209, 214-216.

Vehicles:
Cariole, Norway, 14-15, 52.
Stolkjaerre, 15-16.

Venern, *vay'nern*, Lake, Sweden, 133.

Venice, compared with Stockholm, 135-136.

Vettern, *vet'tern*, Lake, one of most beautiful in Sweden, 133.

Viborg, *vee'borg*, a seaport in Finland, 252-254.

Viken, *vee'ken*, Lake, Sweden, 133.

Vikings, Norsemen of the past, 91-94.
Origin of the name, 92.
Replica of viking ship, 92.
Exploits, 93-94.

Visby, *vis'bü*, city in Sweden:
Building Stone, 221.
Churches, 213-214, 221.
History, 203-207, 209-210, 214-215.
Present importance, 208.

Vordingborg, Denmark, 321

Vöringfos, Norway's grandest waterfall, 23.

Wallenstein, *vahl'len stine*, in the Thirty Years' War, 169.

Waterfalls:
Vöringfos, 23.
Seven Sisters, Geiranger, 64.

Wieselgren, *vee'zel gren*, Peter, originator of the Gothenburg system, 120-122.

"Winter Way," the, international post-road, 232.

Women, Norwegian:
Voters, 13.
Heroism of, 54-55.
Duty and devotion, 55-56 (dairy maid).

Zealand, *zee land*, motor trip through, 317-336.

EGYPT

VENICE
BURTON HOLMES
TRAVELOGUES
LONDON

SWITZERLAND